Successful Business Presentations

Joseph A. Quattrini

TAB BOOKS
Blue Ridge Summit, PA

LIBERTY HALL PRESS books are published by LIBERTY HALL PRESS, a division of TAB BOOKS. Its trademark, consisting of the words "LIBERTY HALL PRESS" and the portrayal of Benjamin Franklin, is registered in the United States Patent and Trademark Office.

First Edition
First Printing
©1990 by TAB BOOKS

Printed in the United States of America

Library of Congress Cataloging-in-Publication Data

Quattrini, Joseph A.
Successful business presentations / by Joseph A. Quattrini.
p.   cm.
ISBN 0-8306-0335-2
1. Business presentations.   I. Title.
HF5718.22.Q38   1990
658.4'52—dc20   89-13489
                                                                  CIP

TAB BOOKS offers software for sale.
For information and a catalog, please contact:

TAB Software Department
Blue Ridge Summit, PA 17294-0850

Questions regarding the content of this book
should be addressed to:

Reader Inquiry Branch
TAB BOOKS
Blue Ridge Summit, PA 17294-0214

Vice President & Editorial Director: David J. Conti
Book Editor: Laurie Miller
Book Design: Jaclyn B. Saunders
Production: Katherine Brown

Contents

for the speakers I've heard who took the time to do it right.

Acknowledgments

The author thanks those who generously shared their professional experience and exemplary materials:

Helen Gurley Brown, Editor, *Cosmopolitan*, 224 West 5th Street, New York, NY 10019.

Mario M. Cuomo, Governor of the State of New York.

George R. Kiley, Kiley Associates, 98 Rock Street, Canajoharie, NY 13317.

L. W. Lehr, Chairman, and John C. Schroeder, Corporate Information and Media Relations, 3M Corporation, 225-5N-04 3M Center, St. Paul, MN 55144-1000.

William E. McCarron, the United States Air Force Academy and The National Council of Teachers of English, 1111 Kenyon Road, Urbana, IL 61801.

F. X. Matt, President, F. X. Matt Brewing Company, 811 Edward Street, Utica, NY 13503.

Mario M. Morino, President, Morino Associates, Inc., 8615 Westwood Center Drive, Vienna, VA 22180-2215.

Victor E. Pesqueira, Manager of Executive Communications, the Xerox Corporation, P.O. Box 1600, Stamford, CT 06904.

Neil Rackham, the Huthwaite Research Group, Wheatland Manor, Route 1, Box 73, Purcellville, VA 22132.

Nancy H. Roberts, Executive Director, Industry—Labor—Education Council, 209 Elizabeth Street, Utica, NY 13503.

Introduction

This book will show you how to become more effective—and therefore more promotable—by making better presentations in formal and informal business speaking situations. You will learn how to assess an audience, define your purpose, organize your presentation, deliver it, and follow it up for success.

WHAT'S SO IMPORTANT ABOUT SPEAKING IN BUSINESS?

The average business person spends about 85 to 90 percent of the working day communicating. If you have to speak to others in order to do your job, this book will help you do it more effectively. If you want to be promotable, you must be able to communicate effectively at every level: with your peers, your superiors, your subordinates, and your customers or clients. You can double your PQ (Promotability Quotient) by becoming a great communicator.

Do you want to advance your career or improve job performance? By showing that you can communicate at all levels, you increase your promotability.

Do you want to build your confidence? When you see that you can perform in pressure situations, you will be ready to take on more challenges and more responsibility.

Do you want to save time and work? You can work smart—which is just as important as working hard—if you use the professional techniques in this book.

Do you want to help in decision-making? You can aid your own decision-making and that of others by organizing information to suit your audience and purpose.

Do you want to increase sales and profits? By getting the job done on the first try, you can increase your own output and that of your department.

Do you want to avoid risk and errors? By planning carefully, you won't make the big mistakes that are seen and remembered by everybody.

Do you want to improve interpersonal relationships? When you are clearly speaking to an audience, they can tell. People like it when you make them feel smart.

WHAT KINDS OF PROBLEMS WILL THIS BOOK HELP YOU SOLVE?

Your Problem: You're told to prepare a report on a project, but not told how long it should be or how much detail should be provided.

Your Solution: Use the *Audience Inventory* to find out exactly what you're hired to do and who will be in the audience.

Your Problem: You know your stuff, but you're not good at organizing it so someone else can understand it or follow it.

Your Solution: Use a *Planning Guide* and *Special Tactics Sheet* to organize the information, plan for the crucial spots in the presentation, and plan for supporting print materials or handouts.

Your Problem: You're assigned to make a type of presentation you've never made before, and you're not sure about the purpose.

Your Solution: Use a Planning Guide to find out the usual purpose of this type of presentation, typical mistakes, and the steps to success for such a presentation.

WHAT WILL YOU LEARN?

This book will show you how to plan, organize, and deliver in these business speaking situations:

- Making a proposal
- Introducing a speaker
- Giving a lecture or keynote address
- Making a demonstration
- Working on a committee
- Giving an oral briefing
- Interviewing
- Negotiating

- Making a telephone sales contact
- Debating or arguing a case
- Working in a discussion group

These include one-way and two-way business presentations, both formal and informal. (Chapter 4 explains one- and two-way situations.)

Instead of describing how effective speakers work, this book shows *you* how to be more effective. You already know how to organize information so it is useful to you—this book shows you how to package it most effectively for the listener or viewer.

Everything you need for a presentation is in Part II in the Planning Guide for that type of presentation. Part I of this book gives a general overview of business speaking situations. Part II goes into each situation in depth, and explains which Planning Guides you need for each situation. Chapter 20, the final chapter, consists of the five groups of forms. It is suggested that you photocopy the forms you will need for each situation. If you desire the forms to fill a standard $8^1/_2$- × - 11-inch sheet of paper, you will need to photocopy the forms at 129%. Each Guide includes everything needed to prepare for the speaking situation—from planning to final evaluation:

1. An explanation of the usual situation, including place, occasion, and audience
2. An analysis of the speaker's purpose
3. An explanation of typical mistakes made in this situation—and how to avoid them
4. The steps to success for planning the presentation
5. An Audience Inventory to help pinpoint the audience's information needs
6. A Pattern Guide to organize the work
7. A Special Tactics Sheet for crucial spots in the presentation
8. An Evaluation Checklist to help to decide if you have "the perfect speech" *before* you give it.

LEARNING FROM PROFESSIONAL LISTENERS

There must be times when you wish you could know exactly what your listener wants to hear. Wouldn't speaking be easier if you could read the minds of your listeners—your client, your boss, your interviewer, or any other audience?

I've asked some important listeners to tell me what they want to hear in a speech, report, briefing, or other presentation. Each chapter in this book will give you formulas for success from such important listeners as:

- Chief executive officers of corporations of all sizes
- Personnel administrators
- Government officials
- Other experienced professionals

Each contributor was chosen because he or she not only has extensive speaking experience, but also extensive listening experience. These "professional listeners" must hear presentations and then make decisions—sometimes, multimillion-dollar decisions—based on what they've heard.

Through their listening experience, they've developed criteria that allow them to quickly judge who is saying something of value and who is wasting their time—and their money.

WHAT RESULTS CAN YOU EXPECT?

By learning from professional listeners and using the tools and techniques described in this book, you can expect your Promotability Quotient to rise. You can expect to build confidence, save time, make better decisions, increase your output, and improve relationships.

When you make dynamic business presentations, you will stand out—in person and on paper—as the one who can solve communication problems, the one who can get the job done.

Part I
How to Do It

1

Promote Yourself

LET'S LOOK AT SOME "CORPORATE" ANSWERS TO THREE QUESTIONS ABOUT business communications:

1. How important is communication in business?
2. How important is business speaking?
3. What speaking skills are needed?

This chapter gives two answers to each question. The first set of answers comes from the Xerox Corporation, a leader among corporate giants. The second set of answers comes from Morino Associates, a firm that specializes in developing and marketing products and services for systems software. This firm represents the majority of corporations—not giant, but diversified and expanding.

Question 1

How Important Is Communication in Business?

Answer #1A—Xerox Corporation

"Management and communication are not separate processes. They are intimately intertwined.

3

"Not to communicate with employees is tantamount to a quarterback not calling a play in the huddle or a conductor not telling the orchestra what piece is being played. The result is chaos.

"The more effectively our people communicate, the more our people feel they will have a stake in the company and its goals. And the more likely, therefore, that Xerox will achieve our ambitious objectives. We need your commitment to this communication effort. In the end it will fail unless all of you, as managers, play a key role.

"When the competition is keen, when the commitment to employee involvement is paramount, it is essential that managers at all levels of Xerox maintain consistent two-way communication."

Answer #1B—Morino Associates

"We work in a fast-paced, dynamic industry where a large part of our success is based on a timely response to the opportunities, events, and trends external to our company."

Question 2

Most people weren't hired to be public speakers. How important is business speaking?

Answer #2A—Xerox Corporation

"Virtually every survey taken on the subject indicates that employees prefer, when possible, to receive information about their work and their company from their manager. And they want their manager to be an authoritative source to answer their questions.

" 'No management team would attempt to operate an organization in today's market conditions and economic climate without a sophisticated capability to communicate with customers, shareholders, and the financial community. In the eighties, it is equally rash for a company to exist without a communications capability fine-tuned to the special needs of employees.' (Arnold R. Deutsch in *The Human Resources Revolution*)

"It will no longer do to let the professionals do [all] the communicating."

Answer #2B—Morino Associates

"Presentations, formal or informal, are the way in which information to support most decision-making processes is provided.

"Our presentations usually take the form of a discussion or strategy meeting, rather than the presentation of one view to a group."

Question #3

What speaking skills are needed to work in industry? What does an effective employee have to be able to do?

Answer #3A—Xerox Corporation

"Everybody at Xerox, from top management on down, is going through a company-wide training program that is fundamentally changing the way we do our work. We're learning how to make our meetings constructive and productive—and how to listen effectively.

"Employee self-esteem, as well as the quality of work life, can only be protected through continuing interpersonal and group communication between them and their manager.

"In their communications with their people, all managers have an obligation to be forthright and timely in discussing objectives, results, problems, difficulties and opportunities."

Answer #3B—Morino Associates

"Morino Associates' corporate culture is, at most times, rather informal. Our meetings are generally aimed toward the round-table discussion rather than formal presentations."

Conclusions

What's happening here? Things are changing. The stakes are higher than they used to be. At one time, an employee who could communicate effectively was an employee who could expect to be promoted. Now, communicating isn't just an advancement skill—it's a survival skill. An employee who can't communicate effectively is an employee who can't work effectively, and who probably won't be an employee for long.

The Xerox Corporation, noting that communication is not an extracurricular activity, but a main activity of work, made a commitment to train all staff to speak and to listen effectively. A report published in 1984 ("High Tech Schools," National Association of Secondary School Principals, Reston, VA) states that U.S. businesses spend about $60 billion annually to train and retrain employees. The training is usually in communication skills.

AT&T spends $6 million per year to teach communication and arithmetic skills to its employees. Because they market information services to other companies, AT&T has a special interest in knowing how offices and people operate. Some interesting statistics are presented in an AT&T advertisement called "Office Automation: How Much Is Too Much?" (AT&T Information Systems, 1985):

- In a typical office, 75 percent of the salary dollars go to managers and professionals.
- The lion's share of time spent in any office is spent communicating: listening, talking, chasing down stray facts, dealing with mail.
- Were you to keep a log, you'd be appalled by how little time you have for actually producing 'work.' (Par for senior executive: about 15 percent.)

WHAT CAN SPEAKING DO FOR YOU?

A large percentage of business communication is spoken, either face-to-face or on the telephone. Speaking can help you to direct the behavior of others, not only to give immediate signals, but also to encourage the growth and development of others. Face-to-face speaking is probably the most effective means of praising, reprimanding, encouraging, or otherwise reacting to other people.

Speaking can help you to get along with others, something necessary for the performance of your job. Setting mutual goals and working to accomplish them requires effective speaking and listening skills. In an office or other work setting where two or more people are not on good speaking terms, there is invariably a slowdown in the flow of work. Others have to work around the noncommunicators, and this means lost time and lost opportunities.

Speaking can help you to learn about yourself and the rest of the world. This learning function might not seem important for business communications, but it is very important. In any discussion involving negotiations or problem solving, the speakers learn by talking—and by listening. In a negotiation, the most important thing you learn about the other person might be the bottom line, the point at which a settlement can be reached. In a problem-solving discussion, several participants might have parts of an idea, and it is only by talking about them that the parts can ever be assembled to make a whole idea, a possible solution to the problem.

These are pretty general statements. Let's be more specific and think about what *you* can get by developing your speaking skills.

What Do You Want?

First of all, think about what you want. Do you want:

- To get an interesting and challenging job?
- To continue to advance within a company?
- To have the freedom to change jobs when you want?
- To have the respect of your colleagues or coworkers?
- To be included in important discussions and negotiations?
- To be able to learn new jobs or responsibilities efficiently?
- To be able to get people to do what you want them to do?
- To be regarded as an interesting person?
- To be somebody that people can talk to?
- To make a good first impression in business and personal situations?
- To be able to take charge of a discussion?
- To be able to sell a product, service, or idea to any audience?

Get What You Want: Achievement and Advancement!

If you want anything on the list above, you can get what you want by developing your speaking skills. The term *public speaking* does not exactly describe the skills you need in most business situations, so I'll use *business speaking* to include the speaking situations common to almost every person in business:

- Giving a briefing or report
- Giving a lecture or demonstration
- Making a sales presentation
- Making a proposal
- Introducing a speaker
- Working with subordinates and superiors
- Working in a discussion group
- Asking and answering questions
- Solving problems
- Interviewing
- Negotiating

Being able to perform with confidence and competence in these business situations means achievement and advancement for you. The rest of this book shows you how to develop versatile, effective speaking skills for the business situations that count.

2

Give the Perfect Speech

EACH OF US WOULD LIKE TO DELIVER THE PERFECT SPEECH, TO MAKE THE PERfect presentation. But what is the perfect speech? Perfection, like beauty, is much valued but hard to define, so I asked for some expert advice from professional listeners. See what conclusions can be drawn about the perfect speech from their answers.

DEFINING THE PERFECT SPEECH

Professional Listener #1—Mario M. Cuomo, Governor of the State o New York.

Mr. Cuomo, highly regarded as a speaker, became known nationally for hi address at the 1984 Democratic National Convention. Here is his view of th perfect speech:

> I've found that defining the elements of a good speech or presentation is a little like trying to define love. The more words you use, the more the ineffable magic you're trying to describe recedes out of view.
> Remember what Yogi Berra is supposed to have said in describing the perfect pitch: 'I can't tell you what it is, but I know it when I see it.' I'm afraid my evaluation of an effective speech would be along those lines: I can't tell you what makes it good, but I know a good speech when I hear one.

9

In truth, I don't believe there is a set formula for a great—or even good—speech. If there were, life would be immeasurably easier for those of us who spend so much time speaking and listening.

Conclusions

1. Forget about defining the perfect speech. There's no set formula for even a good speech or presentation, but the listener can tell a good one from a bad one, whatever you're pitching.
2. In the speaking game, the listeners aren't just spectators—they're the umpires and official scorers, too.

TIME IS MONEY—Make It Easy To Follow

Professional Listener #2—F. X. Matt, President of the F. X. Matt Brewing Company.

As a CEO, Mr. Matt does a certain amount of speaking and has "suffered through a lot of badly made presentations." If you want to make a good presentation to Mr. Matt, just follow this advice:

1. Win my respect, or at least my attention, by being knowledgeable. If you're not knowledgeable, at least give me an example, such as "what I'm going to tell you proved to be useful to A, B, C . . . industries."
2. Simplify the presentation. You're not out to prove that you're the world's most abstruse genius; you want to make a sale.
3. Outline what you're going to say so I know where you're going.
4. Try to avoid jargon and some of the bureaucratic modern words. For example, say *use*, not *utilize*. Say *start up*, not *implement*.
5. Protect my time. Make your presentation brief, not more than fifteen minutes, and let me ask questions if I want to. Actually, if you can present a lot of information to me in a short period of time and get me asking questions, you're moving closer to a sale.

Conclusions

1. "Win my respect . . . simplify the presentation . . . outline what you're going to say . . . protect my time." Add it up: the good presentation is brief, focused and simple, and begins with an outline of itself.
2. Listeners know that time is money, even if speakers don't.
3. When you're speaking, you're always selling something, even if it's just ideas. Don't fall in love with your speech—make your listener fall in love with it.

REMEMBER THE AUDIENCE—Do What You're Hired To Do

Professional Listener #3—Nancy H. Roberts, Former Executive Director of the Private Federation, Industry—Labor—Education Council

Ms. Roberts' job involves constant communication with representatives from all the groups listed in the name of the organization. In an interview I asked her for some evaluation criteria from a listener's point of view.

Q: You've done a great deal of speaking in business situations, but the object of this interview is not so much your speaking experience as your listening experience. I'd like to know your criteria for judging a speech or presentation. What separates the good ones from the bad ones?

A: When I'm listening to a presentation, and I listen to many of them each month, quite often the key is not so much the material as the presentation or delivery of the material. A good speaker will have enthusiasm about the subject, and will get some enthusiasm in return from the audience.

An effective speaker will use many methods to get the point across. You can just tell that the speaker is prepared, is moving from one point to the next according to a plan. The speech or presentation is broken down into proper segments.

First a point will be made, and then the proof or support will follow: an anecdote, incident, illustration, example, etc. And the support should always fit the specific audience. Any joke or personal reference the speaker makes should be relevant to the specific audience—or it should be left out of the speech. An irrelevant joke or story is like an addition to a house that wasn't planned to fit with the original structure. Instead of being an improvement, it's a distraction.

Another point is movement. I like to see speakers move around and show that they have some energy. Gestures come naturally if you're walking around, but they're almost impossible if you're sitting or standing absolutely still at a podium.

When I'm part of the audience, I want to feel that the speaker has come to talk to *me.* You can tell by the flavor of the remarks when a speaker has taken the time to understand the audience. It takes a certain amount of homework to get the necessary background on the audience and situation, but it's always worth it.

Q: How about an evaluation form? Can you give me four or five questions you would use on a speech evaluation form?

A: Here are some questions I'd put on an evaluation form:

1. Did the speech cover the information you expected it to cover?
2. Did the information meet your personal needs? That's a different question from the first one.
3. Were the handouts or support materials helpful?
4. Was it interesting—was the speaker's delivery such that he or she held your interest through the whole speech?

Q: What can you tell me about the listening preferences of CEO's? You deal with many chief executive officers in your work. When they talk about the presentations they have to listen to, what are their complaints?

A: The main one is this: It is a rare speaker (inside or outside of the company) who knows what to say, is able to say it briefly, and is able to document it with proof. If there's going to be a recommendation, it should be made up front, without couching it in fifteen qualifying terms. Even if there's no recommendation, the main point should be the first point of the presentation.

Q: If you had to focus on *one* key piece of advice to speakers, what would it be?

A: Make sure you do what you're hired to do. We've all probably heard enough bad presentations to know what not to do, but the most important thing to do is to make sure you know what is expected of you—and then to do it.

Don't plan a speech by trying to fill the time first and then worrying about giving the audience what they came for. When I hire a speaker I haven't heard before, I always ask for an advance copy of the presentation, so I can be sure the audience is going to get what they expect.

Q: What about in-house presentations or briefings? Sometimes the speaker isn't sure if his or her superior wants just background, a recommendation, or both. How can a speaker in this situation get a clear picture of expectations, and do it without looking foolish—or, worse yet, making a superior look foolish?

A: Ask for the information you need in order to take charge of the speaking situation, but ask for it in a non-threatening way.

You might say something like this: "Let me see if I've got this right," or "Can I send you a draft or an abstract of this before we do it?" Now, you can get the information you need without being threatening, and you can be sure you'll do what is expected of you.

Conclusions

1. A good presentation is one that gets the job done—it meets the audience's needs in an authoritative, interesting manner.
2. A good speaker always finds out what he or she is hired to do, and then does it. The speaker knows what to say, says it briefly, and documents it with proof.

KNOW YOUR STUFF—Be Organized and Complete

Professional Listener #4—Mario M. Morino, President of Morino Associates.

Chapter 1 gave Morino Associates' perspective on business speaking. Here, Mr. Morino contributes his complete guidelines for a presentation. This is a unique look at a CEO's formula for success.

The most important element of any presentation, be it oral or written, is completeness. Completeness can be broken down into several elements:

- Planning
- Presentation basics
- Substantiation
- Summary and wrap-up

Planning. Planning for a presentation is an essential element for its success. Planning may take a few minutes or several hours, but if overlooked, can undermine the success of both the speaker and the presentation.

The planning step includes setting the meeting up, determining the key people who need to be present, developing an agenda for the topics to be discussed, and determining what supporting material should be provided. Planning enables the speaker to think through the presentation from start to end, and anticipate any problems or issues that may arise. "Be prepared" should be the speaker's motto.

Presentation Basics. A person making a presentation need not be a seasoned speaker in order to be successful. While it may be helpful to have some previous presentation experience, even the novice can be very effective if certain steps are followed in the presentation.

1. Always publish an agenda. An agenda serves several purposes. It defines the scope of the presentation, establishes an outline for the meeting,

and helps to keep the meeting "on track" should tangential discussions arise. The agenda should, whenever possible, include a time frame and an allotment of time for each subject to be covered. An agenda gives the speaker an immediate element of control over the meeting.

2. The first few minutes of the meeting are key. Use this time to define a time-frame for the presentation, establish an overview, define objectives, and describe how each area will be addressed in the presentation. This gives the listener a look at the "big picture" of how the meeting will run. Remember it is essential that everyone understand why the presentation is being given and what is to be accomplished as a result.

3. Establish a frame-of-reference. To do this, the speaker should state any assumptions and qualifications made upon which the presentation is based. This is essential to the audience's ability to correctly interpret what is being presented. All too often a presentation puts forth statements or positions which, if not properly qualified, may lead the listener to an entirely different conclusion than the speaker had intended.

4. Speak clearly and concisely. Think about what you want to say and how you are going to deliver your message in advance. All views stated should be well-thought-out and complete. Be prepared. This not only means be prepared to present your planned material, but be equally prepared to deal with the questions from the audience.

5. A presentation should run, at the most, one hour. Ideally, a business presentation should establish the purpose, present the essential ideas, and identify the items to be discussed or for which follow-up action is required, within 20 to 30 minutes. Keep in mind that the attention level of the audience will erode, and it is difficult to maintain focus on the issues in longer presentations.

Substantiation. The speaker must anticipate questions and challenging viewpoints which may arise during the course of his or her presentation. For this reason it is important to have material available which supports, adds to or quantifies the speaker's viewpoint. It is essential that the speaker substantiate his viewpoint and illustrate to the listener a command of his subject.

Summary and Wrap up. A presentation should conclude with a summary and wrap-up. The summary serves to reinforce the major concepts addressed in the presentation, and provide a summary set of recommendations and/or follow-up actions.

Conclusions

1. A good presentation is well planned, brief, and yet complete. The speaker anticipates questions and prepares documentation.
2. A speech is clearly organized into an introduction, which publishes its own agenda; a body of essential ideas; and a conclusion or wrap-up, which summarizes and covers follow-up activities.

SUMMING UP

There may be no perfect presentation. But a good one is complete, brief, focused, organized, documented with evidence, interesting, easy to follow, and relevant to the audience. From the listener's point of view—and the listener is always right—these are the characteristics of a good speech or presentation.

As Mr. Cuomo points out, the listener knows a good presentation after hearing it. Your job, if you want to be an effective speaker, is to know one before the listener hears it. The next chapter shows you how to start by using the speaker's advantages.

3

Use the Speaker's Advantages

HOW DID YOU GET YOUR JOB? DID YOU HAVE AN INTERVIEW? IF YOU'RE LIKE MOST people, you started with paper—application letter and resume—and moved up to a live performance, an interview. As a result of a successful performance in this speaking situation, you were offered a position.

EVALUATING AN INTERVIEW

Like movie and theater critics, interviewers must have standards for judging performances. I asked Mr. George Kiley, an administrator and an experienced interviewer, to explain how he evaluates job applicants in interviews.

Q: You're interviewing people constantly. Can you give me the criteria you use to judge an interview—what you're looking for from the person speaking to you?

A: Within the first few minutes, I'm already going to be tuning in or tuning out, and a lot of this has to do with nonverbal communication. Number one, when a person walks into an interview, I know I'm seeing the best the person has to offer. The person has to have at least as good an appearance as our average employee.

As we start to talk, I'm looking for the person's ability to be relaxed in the situation. I think if the person can't be relaxed one-on-one, then he or she probably won't be able to speak or work very well in a group.

I'm looking for someone who fits into our organization. I don't mean I want everybody to be the same—just the opposite. Part of my hidden agenda is to get a mix of people, a balance of personalities.

Although I might assume basic knowledge from the person's record, I try to find out through the interview the person's ability to communicate that knowledge. I'm also looking for a basic philosophy or attitude toward life and work, because I think they overlap. I don't want somebody who is content to be just vegetating. I want somebody who will dare to take a chance on something new.

As far as actual speaking goes, there are two main points. The person should be able to answer a question—to make a point—without having to use every word in his or her vocabulary to get the point across. I don't want to make two or three trips around the barn to find out what the point is.

The last point is that the person should be able to say it nicely, even if his or her position doesn't agree with mine. It's important to be able to state a position without offending the other person.

Conclusions

1. It's not just what you say, but how you say it.
2. What you don't say may be important, too.
3. In an interview, a person should appear relaxed, friendly, ambitious, and direct and concise.

Mr. Kiley began by saying that the first few minutes are crucial, and that nonverbal communication has a lot to do with his evaluation of a person. Let's see what's involved besides the actual words that are said.

HOW APPEARANCE, TONE, AND EXPRESSION CONVEY MEANING

When you speak, what conveys your meaning? What gets your point across? "Words," you might say. You're partly right.

Communications experts have made various estimates of the importance to meaning of each of these features of a spoken message:

- Physical surroundings
- Dress or attire
- Posture, gestures, and other body language

- Facial expression and eye contact
- Tone, inflection, and loudness
- The words themselves

These estimates have one striking finding in common: they agree that *words account for less than 50 percent of the meaning of a spoken message.*

WHAT IS MEANING?

Let's look at an example of a speaking situation to see how meaning is determined—and by whom. Let's say we are in a business seminar, now, and I am about to make my presentation. I would be communicating many things to you besides the meanings of the words I use. In a way, you'd be "hearing" more than I am saying. Here are five sets of different reactions you might have to my presentation, and none of these "meanings" would be included in my words!

1. The "Meaning" of the Situation

Your Good Reaction: "I must have been chosen for this seminar because they think I'm doing a good job."

Your Bad Reaction: "They stuck me in here because they think I can't do my job. What a waste of time."

2. The "Meaning" of Dress or Attire

Your Good Reaction: "We should dress like that here. That looks comfortable."

Your Bad Reaction: "Doesn't look businesslike. Doesn't he know where he is?"

3. The "Meaning" of Posture and Gesture

Your Good Reaction: "He's pretty brisk and direct, not lounging in his chair."

Your Bad Reaction: "He's awfully tense. He must be new at this."

4. The "Meaning" of Facial Expression

Your Good Reaction: "He looks serious because he wants us to be serious about what we're doing."

Your Bad Reaction: "He must be made of wood. I'll bet his lips won't move when he talks."

These reactions—good or bad—could form before I even opened my mouth! Once these reactions start to add up on the good side or the bad side, it's not very easy to change them.

So far, this is a silent movie. It might seem that sound will improve things. Remember, however, the fate of some of the most popular stars of silent films: when the talkies came, these stars faded quickly. Some didn't speak English, and others had voices that were not pleasing.

Let's see what happens when sound is added to this movie by including the meaning of tone and inflection.

5. The "Meaning" of Tone and Inflection

Your Good Reaction: "Well, he sounds like a real person, not like a record."
Your Bad Reaction: "He's working too hard to come across as one of the guys."

The meaning in tone and inflection comes not from the words themselves but from the way they are spoken. If I were speaking Swedish or any other language you didn't understand, you could still react to tone, inflection, and volume.

The Words

Finally, we come to the sixth area of meaning, the words themselves. As I am speaking, you will have reactions to my choice of words, my style, my ideas, my reasoning and evidence, my organization of the material, and my overall effectiveness as a speaker. However, a good part of that overall effectiveness rating will come not from the words themselves, but from the first five types of reactions.

If, early in the presentation, you decide that I know what I'm doing and that you will get something of value from the program, then I'll be a "good" speaker. On the other hand, if you quickly decide that I'm wasting your time, you'll be unlikely to change your mind, and I'll be a "bad" speaker.

Use these other features of communication to create momentum in a positive direction—the direction of accomplishing your goals. The secret to using these extra channels of communication is to *be prepared,* not only by writing a good manuscript or extensive notes. Each aspect of the presentation, from preliminary research to handling questions after the presentation, should be planned and rehearsed for success.

PLANNING YOUR PRESENTATION

It is normal to be nervous before you make a presentation. *Phonophobia,* fear of speaking in public, consistently ranks high on the list of fears and phobias.

Why do people fear speaking in public? For one thing, speaking involves risk. Something could go wrong, and the stakes could be high. Most business presentations involve matters of importance, with gains or losses as a consequence of the presentation.

Another reason for fear is lack of experience. Most people do not have enough training or experience in public speaking to feel confident and comfortable in front of a group.

The question is not so much how to get rid of the fear as it is how to *use* it. To begin with, realize that fear is a form of tension, and that tension can be put to good purposes. In chapter 2, one of the professional listeners pointed out that a good presentation is an energetic one. Think of tension as a form of energy, and the tension you feel before an important presentation can be turned into the energy you need to keep your audience's attention from start to finish.

Second, start to deal with the fear far in advance of the presentation. Do this by being thoroughly prepared. Once you know exactly what you're doing, you'll be much more confident and at ease. In chapter 2, the president of Morino Associates noted that even an inexperienced speaker can prepare a presentation that is complete, brief, organized, and relevant to the audience. You can make up for a lack of speaking experience by giving yourself the first of the speaker's advantages, the advantage of preparation.

Rehearse for Success

How is rehearsing different from planning? One significant difference is that planning is often a mental process and rehearsing is usually a physical process. Think of yourself as a trapeze artist. Your goal is to achieve a triple somersault. Before you even try the routine with your partner, you might plan for how much time you'll need to spin around three times, at what point you should release the bar, when to come out of the tuck position, and so on.

Then you can start rehearsing. Whether it takes you three tries or three years of trying, you rehearse this move until you can perform it successfully. You make sure that you don't blow it in front of an audience.

In a speaking situation, you want to be every bit as sure. Although inexperienced speakers sometimes think they can "pull out all the stops" for the performance, accomplished speakers are always fully prepared. A simple formula applies:

Planning + Rehearsing = Success

Solid preparation and rehearsal let us use the talents we have to the best effect.

Rehearsing should be extended to every aspect of the speech. An Olympic diving champion was asked about his mental preparation for a complicated dive from the ten-meter (33-foot) platform. He said that, besides practicing for five to six hours daily, he mentally rehearsed each dive before he performed it in competition. He would picture himself approaching the platform, taking off from the edge, turning through the air, entering the water, and finishing the dive under water.

Although the typical speaker does not face a 33-foot drop, the consequences of falling on one's face could be just as severe. If you're going to speak, your rehearsal should cover all features of your presentation. If you must speak from a lectern or podium, you should practice with it. If you're going to use a microphone, practice using it. The same goes for cue cards, a teleprompter, a slide projector, a television camera, a tape recorder, an overhead projector, a chalkboard, a flip-chart, or any other device you might use.

Develop A Fallback Plan

A fallback plan might sound like an escape route to the nearest exit, but it's meant to be used *before* escape is necessary. A fallback plan is a backup to your primary plan. Think of your primary plan as the one you'll use if everything goes your way. The fallback plan comes into play when you can see that your primary plan isn't going to work.

If you have no fallback plan, what will you do if your primary plan doesn't work? You'll be in the same spot as the salesman in this story:

Salesman: Good morning, Madam. Would you have a cup of sugar and some used coffee grounds?

Woman: I think so. Let me check.

Salesman: Could you bring them out here into the living room?. . . (she leaves and returns) . . . Thank you so much. Now, I'll just dump these things on your new rug. I'll add this shovel of dirt that I scooped up from your flower bed. Watch me stamp on the whole mess and grind it in.

Now, madam, comes the Vibralux challenge. If this brand new, ultra-modern, space-saving, high-powered, two-tone Vibralux electric vacuum cleaner with a two-stage motor can't clean up this mess, I'll *eat* everything I've dumped on the floor! Wait! Where are you going?

Woman: To get you a spoon and a napkin. We won't have electricity in this town until next year.

Have more than one fallback plan—one might not be enough.

MY WORST PRESENTATION

My worst experience as a speaker came at a presentation for which I thought I was perfectly prepared. I had a primary plan and a fallback plan. Neither worked.

I had been selected to present a 60-minute workshop on advanced writing techniques to a group of professional educators. Since many workshops were offered at the same time, my audience could range from five to thirty participants. An outline of my program was printed in the conference bulletin so that participants would know what to expect.

My program was based on following the development of a writing plan from the general outline (similar to the Pattern Guide you'll see later) to the finished writing. In order to show the process, I wanted to use overlapping visuals which would show the changes made at each step. The visuals would take the audience from a general "blueprint" to a detailed plan for the writing.

I expected to see about ten participants, so my primary plan was to put my program on computer software. Ten people could easily see the screen and follow the changes. With the software I had designed, I would be able to back up, move ahead, and show the steps rapidly in any sequence. A further advantage would be that I'd need no speaking notes. By referring to the image on the screen, I could run through the entire performance without being tied to notes.

My fallback plan was based on the same principle of overlapping visuals. I knew that if more than ten or twelve people attended my presentation, the computer screen would be too small to serve the audience. Plan B was to use a series of transparencies on an overhead projector. These would be a little less flexible than the computer program, but either plan would free me from notes. Nor would participants need to fumble with a fifty-page handout while trying to follow my presentation. Each participant would receive a three-page handout— not to read, but to use for the writings to be completed during the workshop.

I visited the physical setting and found that the conference rooms were large enough for fifty people. The actual room I was assigned was being used, but the rooms were all alike, so I walked through one, tried the screen, and tried the microphone.

For the twentieth time, I checked my materials and equipment: handouts, computer and software, projector and spare bulb, extension cords, rolling cart, and all. I had everything; everything worked. What could go wrong?

Forty people showed up. I scratched the primary plan and began to set up the overhead. Even with forty people, everyone would be able to see.

Click. Click. I'm clicking the switch, but the power-driven screen won't come down. Okay, no reason to panic. We'll get a portable screen.

None available. Okay, we'll show it on the wall.

We could, but the walls are covered with textured wallpaper in a geometric design. Projected on the wallpaper, even the simplest of my transparencies looked like a wiring diagram for a 747. I was thinking that this would have been funny if it had been happening to someone else—Peter Sellers, maybe, in a movie.

There were very few laughs. Without the visuals on which my program depended, people could not see what to do. Trying to *tell* them what to do was like trying to tell someone over the telephone how to tie shoelaces.

I had a plan, and I had a fallback plan. And I had sixty minutes of intense embarrassment in front of forty people, some of them my colleagues.

I don't think my horror story is an uncommon one. If you've done much speaking, you must have at least one, also. Use foresight to set up your fallback plan (or plans) by thinking of what can go wrong with your primary plan. Make sure your fallback plan isn't too much like the primary plan, or the same problem may cripple both plans.

Start With "What If?"

You don't have to cover every possible contingency. If there's an earthquake or a nuclear war, your audience probably won't be interested in the rest of your presentation anyway. Do try to cover the major "what if's":

- What if the physical setting is changed?
- What if the audience is smaller or larger or smarter or meaner or somehow different from what you expected?
- What if the support materials are lost or destroyed, or don't work?

The fallback plan should be simpler than the primary plan, and should probably lead to a shorter presentation, as well. By the time you know you need the fallback plan, you'll probably have lost some time and energy. The audience may have lost some of their attentiveness, also, so the fallback plan should make things easy for everyone. When you rehearse, rehearse the fallback plan, also. It may be your only safety net, and you'll want to be sure that it works.

SUMMING UP

So far, this book has shown you:

- How important speaking is in business communications
- What effective speaking can do for you
- What makes the perfect speech
- The channels of communication in a typical speaking situation.

Chapter 4 discusses business presentations as business transactions.

4

Get Ready for the Speaking Transaction

WHAT IS THE TOUGHEST AUDIENCE IN THE WORLD? YOUR BOSS? YOUR EMPLOYEES? Stockholders? Your clients? The public? The government?

I don't think there is a toughest audience. Any audience can be tough on a speaker—and should be—if the speaker doesn't give them what they want and need for their purposes.

UNDERSTAND THE SPEAKING TRANSACTION

Think of a business presentation as a *transaction*—as an exchange for the mutual benefit of two parties. Even if one side is doing all the speaking, there is another side out there: the audience. Without their participation—not just their physical presence, but their participation—no speaker can be successful.

There's no such thing as a captive audience. Even if people have to sit there until you're through speaking, they don't have to pay attention to you or to believe you. In this sense, all business speaking is *persuasive*, and the first thing you have to do is persuade the audience that they should listen to you.

The Speaker's Wants

- I want the audience to give me their attention all the way through the speech.
- I want them to trust me and to believe that I know what I'm talking about.
- I want them to follow my line of reasoning.
- I want them to agree with me.
- I want them to follow a course of action (buy the product, etc.).

The Audience's Wants

- I want this presentation to hold my interest from start to finish.
- I want the speaker to be honest, knowledgeable, organized, and clear.
- I want the speaker to respect my intelligence and understand my background.
- I want the speaker to *speak to me*—to give me the information and ideas that I need.
- I want to be able to make the right decision based on what I've heard.

As a speaker, keep in mind that the audience has a *wants* list that's at least as long as your own. Remember that you can succeed only by meeting the audience's needs.

Let's see how you can plan your speech to get what *you* want by giving the audience what *they* want. If you look at the items that appear on both wants lists, you can see the common ground that already exists in the speaking situation. Even in the most bitterly opposed negotiating circumstances, there are always areas of common ground or mutual interest.

Think of these areas as natural bridges, and then use them as such. Why spend your audience's time building a bridge if you can use one that already exists? Here are the natural bridges in a speaking situation. They come from both sides of the wants lists.

1. Interest and clarity
2. Integrity
3. Organization and reasoning
4. Needed information

You can use these natural bridges to match your speaking purposes—your wants—with the wants of your audience.

Target Your Purposes

Think, for a moment, about how many purposes you have in a given speaking situation. Even if you're making a brief report to your immediate superior, you have many purposes, some of them unspoken. Let's say the specific purpose of the report is to tell how sales are going with a new product. You'll also want to show your boss that you're a competent and valuable employee who can handle responsibility, you're knowledgeable about your subject, you're prepared, and so on.

I call these *unspoken purposes* because most of us do not go to the boss and say, "See what a valuable employee I am?" Yet that is exactly what most people would like the boss to conclude.

This book does not deal directly with these unspoken purposes. There's a good reason for this: you can accomplish your unspoken purposes *only* by accomplishing the direct purposes of your report. If your boss can't tell from your report whether sales went up or went down or stayed the same, then you're not going to appear to be competent, valuable, knowledgeable, or thorough.

This book focuses on the business purposes of a speaking situation, starting with providing the information your audience needs. If your presentation doesn't provide needed information, it won't matter how interesting and honest and clear and well organized you are.

Get the Right Level of Information

How can you determine what is necessary information? Let's start by defining the term *necessary*. Necessary information is the information your audience needs to accomplish their purposes. You usually cannot interview your audience before the presentation to find out their backgrounds, experience, and specific interests, but you can analyze your audience to plan for success. During your presentation you should *look at* your audience, but during your planning you should try to *see* your audience. The following *Audience Inventory* will help you to match up your wants with the wants of the audience.

AUDIENCE INVENTORY

Type of Presentation: _____

Size and Makeup of Audience: _____

1. Who are these people? What is their background in this business or technical area?

2. What is their experience in this area?

3. What are their special interests? What do they want from me?

4. What are my purposes? What do I want to give them?

5. How can I match up these wants lists?

***

6. What do they know about the company (or other group) I represent?

7. What do they know about my background, experience, and professional reputation?

***

8. How are they likely to react to my ideas on this issue or proposal? Will they be likely to agree? To what extent?

9. What kinds of evidence would be most convincing to them?

10. What level of detail should be included?

***

11. How are they accustomed to getting information? How long will they want to listen?

12. How would they want the material organized? Where would they want me to begin?

***

13. What do they have to be able to do on the basis of the information and arguments I present?

14. Should they be aware of a trend? Able to draw a conclusion? Able to make a decision?

***

15. What questions will they be likely to ask?

You may have to do some research to get answers to these questions, or you may be able to answer them from your own knowledge. In any case, you need to match your speaking purposes with your analysis of your audience. The more you can determine about your audience's "wants," the more likely you are to be successful in your speaking.

Match Up the Wants Lists

Start with what the audience already knows about the topic. To that, add what else they want to know. Then, match up the audience's list with your own list. Add what you want the audience to know, and you'll have a good picture of the information needs for a given speaking situation. To pinpoint what you want them to know, you'll have to define your speaking purpose carefully.

THE OTHER SIDE OF THE TRANSACTION: The Speaker's Purpose

Your speaking purpose is the controlling feature for planning any presentation. You want to make sure you get what is on *your* wants list. From your standpoint, your presentation can be evaluated by how well you accomplished your purpose.

It may seem like oversimplifying to say that a presentation has only a single purpose, but I think it is necessary to define a primary purpose and then to focus the presentation on that purpose.

I've never heard an audience complain that a speech was too clear or too easy to understand, so the best editing advice is to *simplify*. That's also the best *planning* advice. The speaker who gets involved in a maze of purposes is likely to lose sight of the main one. If you don't accomplish your main purpose, how good can your presentation be?

THE THREE LEVELS OF PURPOSE

Defining your primary purpose and organizing the presentation can be done at the same time if you know the organizing pattern to use for your situation. There are three levels of speaking purpose and there are organizing patterns for each level. Here are the three levels of purpose:

Level One: Speaking to present facts
Level Two: Speaking to draw conclusions
Level Three: Speaking to recommend an action

Level One is the least demanding, as it requires only the facts. A Level-One report on an inventory, for example, would be little more than a statistical summary—facts with no conclusions or recommendations attached.

A Level-Two report is more demanding. A Level-Two report on the inventory would be based on facts, but the facts would not be the most important part of the report. The most important part of the report would be the conclusion drawn from the facts. The conclusion might be something like this: "We're keeping far too much inventory on hand for our production purposes."

A Level-Three report on the inventory would include facts, conclusions, and a recommendation for action. In this report, the recommendation for action would be the most important part. The recommendation for the inventory report might look like this: "Start reducing our inventory."

You will not be asked to make very many Level-One reports in business situations. If all the audience wants is the facts, there's no need to take the time to listen to a spoken report. A written report probably does the job more efficiently. (Chapter 7 looks at the relationship between written reports and spoken reports.)

Most of your business presentations will be at Level Two or Level Three, and there will probably be more at the action level. This should not be surprising. Business runs on actions, not on ideas. After a report is made, someone usually has to make a decision and carry out an action.

Here are some examples of Level-Three situations and the actions the speaker might want to result.

Situation	Action Recommended
Employment interview	Hire me.
Sales presentation	Buy this.
Solution proposal	Do it this way.
Marketing proposal	Start the sales campaign.

In each case the recommended action is the payoff, the primary purpose for making the presentation. It is the most important part of a Level-Three presentation.

THE ORGANIZING SECRET—Use Patterns of Communication

The following shows the outlines for some organizing patterns for each level of purpose. After you analyze your audience and define your primary purpose, you can select the best pattern to organize your presentation. The pattern will help you to block out your main ideas in a useful sequence before you worry about the number of details or the exact wording.

Level One: Statement-Support

Statement:	States a general fact or facts
Support #1:	Gives details which support the statement
Support #2:	Gives more supporting details
Support #3:	Gives more details
Application:	Restates the main point

Level Two: Thesis-Proof and How-To

Thesis-Proof

Thesis:	States a conclusion or interpretation which must be proven
Proof #1:	Gives evidence to prove the conclusion
Proof #2:	Gives additional evidence

| Proof #3: | Gives additional evidence |
| Significance: | Gives the consequences or importance of the conclusion |

How-To

Motivation:	Tells the importance of the process being explained
Step #1:	Gives the first step of the process
Step #2:	Gives the next step
Step #3:	Gives the last step
Application:	Tells how and when this process can be used

Level Three: Opinion-Reason and Problem-Solution

Opinion-Reason

Opinion:	States an opinion about an action
Reason #1:	Gives a reason to support the opinion
Reason #2:	Gives another reason
Reason #3:	Gives another reason
Recommendation:	Recommends a specific course of action

Problem-Solution

Problem:	Defines the problem
Effects:	Lists the results or symptoms of the problem
Causes:	Traces the causes
Solution:	Offers a solution strategy
Significance:	Tells the benefits of this solution

Although each of these outlines shows five pattern parts, the number of parts can be changed to suit your needs. If you're using the Opinion-Reason pattern to argue a position, you can use two reasons or four or any other number you need.

Suit Pattern to Purpose

Let's match the speaking situations mentioned so far with patterns that will organize the presentations effectively.

Introducing a Speaker: Statement-Support pattern.
This is primarily a matter of giving relevant information about the speaker.

Giving a Lecture or Address: Pattern will vary with purpose.
Since a lecture or address could be at any level of purpose, no single pattern can be recommended.

Making a Proposal/Offering a Solution Strategy: Opinion-Reason or Problem-Solution.
These are always Level-Three speaking situations, since the desired outcome is action from the audience.

Giving a Demonstration/Giving Directions: How-To.
The How-To pattern is perfect for explaining or demonstrating how to do something.

Giving a Report or Briefing: Statement-Support, Thesis-Proof.
Although reports vary in purpose, they will probably be at Level One or Level Two.

Interviewing/Making a Telephone Presentation: Opinion-Reason, Problem-Solution.
If you are interviewing for a position, you are involved in a Level-Three situation, as your purpose in interviewing is to get the job. A telephone sales presentation is also a Level-Three situation.

Brainstorming/Problem-Solving: Problem-Solution.
Brainstorming is a part of problem solving. The purpose of brainstorming is to gather ideas about causes or solutions or significance, but the ultimate purpose, solving the problem, is a Level-Three situation.

Working in a Discussion Group or Panel: Pattern varies with purpose.
The nature of the discussion dictates the choice of organizing pattern.

Debating/Arguing a Case/Negotiating: Problem-Solution, Opinion-Reason.
The purpose of debating or arguing is usually to win, so Level-Three patterns

will most often be used. The anticipated outcome of negotiation is always an action or actions.

The patterns I've suggested are certainly not the only means of organizing such presentations. These patterns are, in my view, the choices that best fit the purposes and situations described.

The Advantages of Using Patterns

Here are a few of the advantages of using patterns to plan and organize your presentations:

1. *Efficiency.* By using a pattern, you can prepare much more quickly. The pattern organizes the major parts of the speech for you, and you won't spend hours trying to revise a disorganized presentation. As soon as you select a pattern, you've organized the main segments of your work.

2. *Completeness.* Selecting a pattern establishes the requirements of all the parts of the speech. For example, if you use Opinion-Reason to organize a proposal, you can't forget to make a recommendation—it's part of the pattern outline.

3. *Focus.* Because you'll start organizing the presentation with your primary purpose in mind, you'll never lose sight of it—nor will your audience. The main point will be clearly made at the beginning and at the end of your presentation.

4. *Flexibility.* You can easily adjust the length or complexity of the speech when you use a pattern. You can do this while you are planning the presentation or while you are giving it. With a pattern, you can add or omit details without ever losing the main ideas.

5. *Ease of Learning.* Using patterns is second nature when using language. Memory books offer all kinds of devices to help people remember details, but the devices are all based on linking the details with something familiar and easy to remember. Your memory device will be the pattern you use. Follow the pattern outline to keep track of where you are in your presentation—without resorting to reading from a manuscript.

    Most listeners don't want a speaker to read to them. Nor do they want to listen to a robot who has memorized a presentation but forgotten that there is a live audience. Using a pattern outline for your speaking notes allows you to stay in contact with your audience.

6. *Ease of Listening.* Your introduction helps your audience recognize your

pattern of organization. Once they do this, they can easily follow your line of reasoning, because they can anticipate where you are going. (Chapter 6 shows how to give your audience the plan of your presentation.) The same pattern that serves as a memory aid for you when you give the speech can serve as a listening aid for your audience. It gives them a structure to follow, a road map of your ideas.

Now, let's see how the concept of pattern fits into the entire speech transaction. As a speaker, you have a list of wants which can be condensed to a primary purpose for speaking. You may wish to present facts (Level One), draw conclusions (Level Two), or recommend an action (Level Three).

Your audience has a list, also, which you try to determine with the Audience Inventory. You select the pattern that is most likely to get you what you want by giving the audience what they want. This pattern will be used to organize the ideas and details in your presentation.

IDENTIFY THE SPEAKING SITUATION

The next factor to consider is the speaking situation: what are the circumstances of your speech or presentation? *Speech* and *presentation* are words that cover many different circumstances. This book organizes speaking situations, regardless of purpose, into two groups. The division is based on the flow of information, which can be one-way or two-way.

THE ONE-WAY SITUATION

In some cases, the flow of information is a more important factor than is the size of the audience. Let's say you must prepare a five-minute audio tape on how to make telephone sales calls. Whether your tape is heard by one person in a listening booth or is broadcast through an entire auditorium, the flow of information is the same. The flow is one-way, and the order of information is predetermined when the tape is recorded. Each playing of the tape will give the same result. In this extreme instance, the speaker is not even present at the time of the speech. There are many other situations, however, where the spoken communication is mostly one-way:

- Introducing a speaker
- Making a proposal
- Giving a lecture or keynote address
- Making a demonstration

- Giving a status or committee report
- Giving orders or directions
- Giving a briefing

In these circumstances, you, as the speaker, will be doing most of the talking. With the exception of questions from the audience, the floor is yours. Information goes from you to the audience, and there is little spoken feedback or response.

THE TWO-WAY SITUATION

In two-way situations, information (in the form of speech) flows from you to another person or other people, and flows from this audience back to you. You are talking with rather than talking to an audience. Two-way situations include:

- Negotiating/Interviewing and being interviewed
- Brainstorming and solving problems
- Working in a discussion group or panel
- Making a telephone sales call
- Debating an issue or arguing a case

In two-way situations, you can be a speaker without being the focus of attention at all times. You know that another person (or other people) will be speaking also, and that part of your job is going to be to listen and then to respond to their words.

I don't think it's possible to say if two-way communication is harder or easier than one-way communication. They are different and require slightly different planning and delivery strategies. The main difference is the *immediacy of feedback*. In one-way situations, there is likely to be little spoken feedback. In two-way situations, you know you can get immediate spoken feedback—even if you don't want it. Let's look at a few familiar examples.

A business letter is essentially a one-way communication. You hope to get the response you want, but you don't expect to get it while you are writing the letter. In contrast, a telephone call is a two-way situation. The other party can give a response immediately, and can even interrupt you to ask questions or give other reactions. If you're expecting a two-way situation, you might be surprised in some cases.

What happens when you make a business telephone call expecting to speak with someone, and you end up speaking to the other person's answering machine? Your speaking plan called for a two-way situation, but you're in a one-way situation. You can't have a discussion and you can't answer questions. Your message will probably be limited to thirty seconds. You have to decide whether to try to leave a message or just to give your name and telephone number. If you *planned* to call and give a thirty-second message to a machine, there would be no problem.

Let's reverse the situations. Let's say the caller expects to speak to an answering machine, and wants the other party to return the call on the next business day. What happens if the other party happens to be in the office and picks up the phone? The speaker's one-way plan isn't appropriate for this two-way situation, and confusion is likely to result.

MASTER THE SITUATIONS

When you're speaking, most surprises are likely to be unpleasant ones. It is best to be prepared for more than one speaking situation, more than one type of audience, and more than one type of response. You'll need a primary plan and a fallback plan to use when you can see that the primary plan isn't working.

For each situation listed below, there will be a complete Planning Guide in Part II of this book. You'll see how to use your introduction to give your audience the plan of your speech, how to use written materials and visual aids to help to convey your message, and how to use other methods to ensure your success.

Right now, we'll look at some one-way speaking situations to see how the information flow influences the speaking-listening transaction. The following diagram shows the general flow of information in most one-way speaking situations.

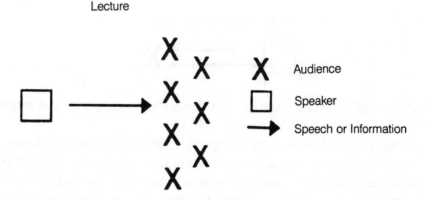

Lecture

X
  X   X   Audience
X   X   □   Speaker
X X   →   Speech or Information
X   X
  X

This is the usual flow for lectures, addresses, introductions, proposals, briefings, reports, directions, and instructions. For a demonstration, the flowchart or diagram is only slightly different.

Demonstrations

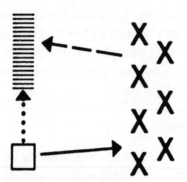

The flowcharts illustrate that information goes from speaker to listener in a one-way situation. It is important to remember that a one-way situation may also be a one-chance situation. The audience is going to have only one chance to get the point, and you're going to have only one chance to accomplish your purpose. You have to build in extra chances—for your audience and for yourself—in one-way situations.

Two-way situations, those which are likely to include immediate feedback or response, show a different information flow. For interviews and telephone conversations, which generally involve only two people, the flowchart looks like this:

Interviewing or Telephoning

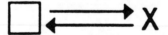

Speaker and listener change roles in these situations, sometimes without agreement on whose turn it is to speak.

Brainstorming and problem-solving usually involve more than two people. In addition, they have purposes which are different from telephoning or interviewing. The primary purpose of brainstorming is to bring out and record as many ideas as possible on the subject at issue. All ideas or suggestions are accepted, and the merits of individual ideas are not discussed during brainstorming. Following is a flowchart for brainstorming.

Brainstorming

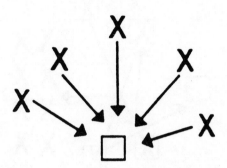

Brainstorming is an early step of problem-solving. For example, the focal point of a brainstorming session may be a problem: How can we improve communications within the company? After a great many ideas are recorded from the brainstorming session, the problem-solving can continue. In this process, however, the list of suggestions or possible solutions is narrowed until a workable plan can be developed. A flowchart for problem-solving might look like this:

Problem-solving

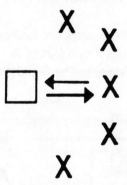

A discussion group works in much the same way, although the subject may not always be a problem, and the outcome may not always be a solution strategy. A panel discussion, a more complicated situation, might be diagrammed like this:

Panel discussion

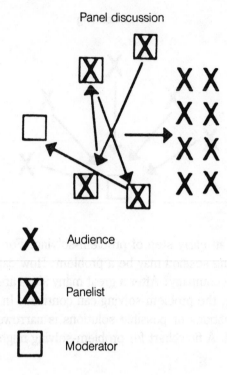

X   Audience

⊠   Panelist

☐   Moderator

Here, there are several levels of audience. If you are a member of a panel, you may be speaking directly to another panel member, but indirectly to the rest of the audience.

Debating or arguing a case is similar to being on a discussion panel, except that the outcome is usually judged by a part of the audience. In a debate or case argument, there is usually a winner. The flowchart might look like this:

Debate

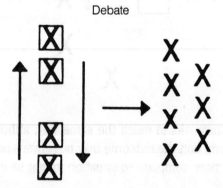

Negotiating, a much more common two-way situation, is a special case. If there are only two sides to the negotiation, and only one person representing each side, then the flowchart would look like this:

Negotiating

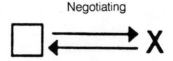

However, negotiations are often more complicated. There may be three or more sides involved. There may be chief negotiators who head teams for each side. The negotiators at the table may not be empowered to make important decisions on the spot, so many meetings and reports may be required before an agreement can be reached. Although no "winner" may be declared, both sides will be keeping score for the life of the agreement reached.

In negotiating, as in all two-way situations, you have to anticipate the type of feedback or response you will get to each part of your presentation. Then you have to be ready to handle those responses.

PLANNING GUIDES

Part II of this book contains *planning guides* for each of the one-way and two-way situations just described. Each guide includes the following materials:

- An explanation of the usual situation, including place, occasion, and audience
- An analysis of the speaker's purpose
- An explanation of typical mistakes made in this situation—and how to avoid them
- The steps to success for planning your presentation
- An Audience Inventory
- A Pattern Guide to organize your work
- A Special Tactics sheet to plan the crucial spots in a presentation
- An Evaluation Checklist to check your presentation and revise it, if necessary, before you give it

We've seen diagrams and brief descriptions of different one-way and two-way speaking situations. Chapter 5 gives a more detailed analysis of what's going on in a speaking situation.

5

Know the
Dynamics of Discussions

IN CHAPTER 1 YOU SAW THAT THE XEROX CORPORATION WAS MAKING A HUGE commitment—in time and money—to improve communications within the company. The chief goal was to make meetings more productive and efficient by improving people's speaking and listening skills.

You saw that Morino Associates' success in a fast-paced and competitive field depended on the ability to give, in the president's words, "... a timely response to an opportunity." The key to developing the timely response was the round-table discussion or strategy meeting.

One point seems clear: in business, *meetings are important speaking situations*. Further, listening is more than simply hearing, and speaking is more than simply talking. Let's take a look at what really happens in a meeting where ideas are discussed.

INITIATE, REACT, AND CLARIFY

The companywide program for Xerox was developed by the Huthwaite Research Group, a Virginia-based consulting firm. In order to develop an effective program for Xerox, Huthwaite had to be able to answer these questions:

1. What kinds of behavior are involved in a discussion?

2. What distinguishes high performance (or productivity) from low perform-ance in a discussion situation?

3. How can people develop their skills to become more effective and make meetings more productive?

The answers to questions one and two are not simple, nor did they come quickly. The following paragraphs, reprinted with permission from Huthwaite, are taken from the training program for Xerox. They show the conclusions drawn about productive behavior in discussions or meetings.

WHAT IS BEHAVIOR ANALYSIS?

Behavior analysis is the process of studying behavior in order to compare and evaluate its effectiveness in various situations.

All kinds of behavior can be studied. However, for our purposes we will focus on verbal behavior—spoken words.

If you wanted to identify the verbal behaviors that distinguish high per-formance in a particular situation from low performance, you would find some performers of both types and gather information about their interac-tions with others.

You might record all that they said and classify each statement accord-ing to its type. Then you could count the number of times each person used each type of statement. From this data, you might find some differences that would help others to pattern their behavior to resemble that of the suc-cessful people.

Fortunately, some extensive research has been conducted on the verbal behavior of people in group meetings and discussions. You are in the posi-tion of being able to use the results of this research to shape your own behavior toward a pattern that is likely to increase your effectiveness.

WHO DID THE RESEARCH?

Beginning in the late 1960s and continuing through the mid-1970s, large-scale research was carried out by the Huthwaite Research Group in an attempt to develop a truly descriptive and useful system for classifying behavior. This was a long and tedious process, because the number of potential behavior categories is almost infinite. The researchers finally con-cluded that a meaningful list of categories could be produced if each of the selected behaviors categories met five basic criteria:

1. It could be measured accurately.

2. It was easy to understand.

3. It was distinct from other categories.
4. People could change how often they used it.
5. It could be related to effectiveness of performance.

WHAT CATEGORIES OF BEHAVIOR WERE IDENTIFIED?

Finally, eleven behavior categories were identified that met these criteria. The researchers named them:

- proposing
- building
- supporting
- disagreeing
- defending/attacking
- seeking information
- giving information
- summarizing
- testing understanding
- bringing in
- shutting out

After the behavior categories were developed, a large-scale study was undertaken to see how they applied to task-oriented situations. The results showed that there are three main classes of behavior important to any discussion about solving a problem or completing a task. They are:

Initiating: behaviors which put forth ideas, concepts, suggestions, or courses of action,

Reacting: which constitute an evaluation of other people's contributions, and

Clarifying: behaviors which exchange information, facts, opinions, and other clarification.

HOW DO THE ELEVEN BEHAVIOR CATEGORIES FIT INTO THESE THREE MAIN CLASSES?

Nine of the eleven behavior categories can be assigned to one of the three main classes. *Bringing in* and *shutting out* are special process categories.

Initiating	**Clarifying**	**Reacting**
Proposing	Seeking information	Supporting
Building	Giving information	Disagreeing
	Summarizing	Defending/attacking
	Testing understanding	

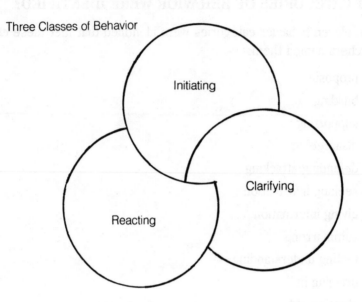

Three Classes of Behavior

Figure 5-1 represents the way the three main classes of behavior fit together in effective discussions. All three are important. Their purposes are interlocking.

There is no universal perfect proportion of use of the three classes of behavior. Situations vary. Some discussions benefit from more of one class of behavior than another.

But effective discussions need some of each kind of behavior. Discussions that get locked into one or two types of behavior tend to get more and more unbalanced with negative consequences on the discussion.

WHAT EFFECTS DO EACH OF THE THREE CLASSES OF BEHAVIOR HAVE ON A DISCUSSION?

Initiating

- Puts ideas out for consideration
- Creates enthusiasm
- Orients to future action

Discussions with few initiating behaviors tend to get bogged down in detailed analysis of a limited number of ideas and get boring. However, a discussion with too much initiating may get so dispersed that it also fails to get anything accomplished.

Reacting

- Lets people know what others are thinking
- Helps get information out
- Facilitates open communication

Discussions with few reacting behaviors feel closed and awkward. They tend to get repetitious. However, overuse of reacting behaviors may result in emotional discussions with conflicts and misunderstanding.

Clarifying

- Increases clarity and mutual understanding
- Fosters deeper analysis of issues
- Encourages exchange of ideas

Discussions that are low in clarifying behavior may become disorganized. Hasty decisions may be made that are not fully understood by the participants. However, too much clarifying behavior can result in a discussion using up a lot of time without much progress. The discussion may get stuck on minor details.

In summary:

- Each of the three main classes of behavior are needed for a successful discussion.
- Using any of the classes to excess or scarcity can have a detrimental effect on the meeting.
- The best balance will vary by the type of discussion being held.
- The most appropriate use of behaviors within each of the main classes also varies by the situation and the desired outcome.

CONCLUSIONS FOR BUSINESS SPEAKERS

Huthwaite's research supports the idea that, in a discussion or meeting, you can't be an effective speaker without also being an effective listener. Initiating, reacting, and clarifying behaviors are all required for productive meetings.

As was true in our discussion of the perfect speech, there is no single formula for the perfect meeting or discussion. Understanding the three main classes of behavior, however, can help you to plan your own contributions in these speaking situations so that you can be a productive member of a productive group. Chapters 16 and 17 describe how to make your discussion and brainstorming groups more productive. But for now, chapter 6 explains how to give your audience—in any situation—the plan of your speech, and then how to keep their attention.

6

Show Them the Plan—and Keep Their Attention

THE FOLLOWING ADVICE ON EFFECTIVE SPEAKING COMES FROM AN INTERVIEW with Mr. L. W. Lehr, the former CEO of 3M Corporation

I listen to a lot of presentations and reports. The good ones, the effective ones, usually have a few things in common. The ideal presentation is brief, clear and to the point . . . without a lot of puff and salesmanship.

The speaker gets right to the point, without much preamble, and tells the audience what they're going to hear in the next few minutes.

Then come the *facts:*

- *What*   Describe the subject or issue and its relevance.
- *Where*   Pinpoint locations involved or affected.
- *Why*   Be clear about the reasons for or against an action. Are they good business reasons? In the community or national interest? Or do they serve someone's personal interests?
- *Who*   Be clear about who will be responsible for taking what actions.

- *When*   Set target for when an action is to take place and when results will be known.

Finally, a presenter should sum up, then present his or her conclusions and recommendations clearly and straightforwardly.

A speaker like this has far more impact than one that is either afraid to make his or her point too clearly, or far too eager to sell a point of view.

Did you notice that the way Mr. Lehr presents this information shows the *plan* of presentation? A single glance shows you not only the introduction, body, and conclusion, but also the organization within the body—the *what, where, why, who,* and *when.*

If this information were shown to a listening audience through a printed handout or a visual aid (chart or overhead transparency), the audience could easily keep track of the speaker's progress.

MAKE A PATTERN GUIDE

How does such organization help? Organized information is easier to read, easier to listen to, and easier to use. This chapter describes several ways to *show* your listening audience the plan of your speech—and then to keep them with you during its presentation.

The most efficient method of showing the plan is by using a pattern outline or *pattern guide* in one or more of these ways:

1. As an overview in the introduction to your speech
2. As a printed handout
3. As a chart, overhead transparency, or other visual

Using Your Pattern Guide as an Overview

If you condense your speech so that each pattern part is expressed in one sentence, you'll have a five-sentence overview. With a little work, you can further condense these sentences into one or two which you can deliver in less than one minute. Here is an example of a one-sentence overview of a Problem-Solution speech about a proposed expansion into new products:

"After we see the stagnating effects (*problem* and *effects*) of being a one-product company (*cause*), we'll look at a plan to diversify (*solution*) and become more dynamic (*significance*)."

Give this type of overview in the introduction, and your audience can follow this mental outline through the rest of the speech.

Using Your Pattern Guide as a Printed Handout

If you don't trust invisible mental outlines, or if your presentation is a detailed one, make your outline visible. Fit it neatly on one sheet of paper, and distribute it before or at the beginning of your speech. Pattern Guide sheets can be used to construct handouts that are easy to read in a minute or less. Here is a pattern guide for a solution to a problem with overloaded printers.

Problem	At some times during the day there is a 30-minute wait to get access to a printer.
Effects	A lot of time is being wasted because the printers are holding up everything else.
Causes	Everyone tries to use the printers during peak times, an hour before lunch and an hour before the end of the day.
Solution	Schedule printer use in various time blocks.
Significance	Everyone will have rapid access to printers during his or her scheduled use time, and there'll be no interruption of the flow of work.

Using Your Pattern Guide as a Visual

Put your outline on a flipchart, overhead, or other type of visual so that you and your audience can refer to it during the course of your speech. If you've practiced enough, you can use the visual outline as your speaking notes, and avoid looking down and losing eye contact with your audience.

PREPARE LISTENERS FOR YOUR CONCLUSION

Let's say you've given an overview and you're off to a good start in your presentation. You've passed the first critical spot, the introduction, and you've captured the attention of the audience. Another critical spot comes at the end of the body of the presentation. If you've given only a spoken overview, you'll want to give your audience another look at it before coming to your conclusion, the bottom line of the presentation.

At the start of your conclusion—just before the Application, Significance, Solution, or Recommendation—give the pattern outline again. This allows you to summarize what you've already covered and then lead directly into your final point, your last chance with the audience.

Summarizing should take less than a minute, and should signal the audience that the important conclusion is coming up. Even in short presentations, there are psychological low spots for the audience, places where attention starts to fade. This summary can recapture their full attention when you need it—when you are about to get to the bottom line.

Here is a summary for the Problem-Solution presentation mentioned earlier in this chapter.

"We've seen how our growth potential is limited (*problem* and *effects*) by being a one-dimensional company (*cause*); now, let's look at a way to develop added dimensions (*solution*) and to become a dynamic, expanding part of the industry (*significance*)."

We've identified the introduction and conclusion as being especially important parts of a presentation, your best opportunities with the audience. Let's go another step. Even these parts have parts: there's a beginning to an introduction (the opening words) and a close to a conclusion (the final words).

GET THE FIRST WORD IN: Create Focus

Your first words, the first minute of your speech, can establish you as being competent and confident, or neither of these. Besides establishing that you're worth listening to, you want the opening of your presentation to focus audience attention on your main point. Here are six ways to focus attention on you and your main point. These also appear on the Special Tactics sheets you will use in Part II.

1. Use a focus object
2. Use deliberate silence
3. Use an anecdote, fable, or story
4. Use a familiar quotation
5. Cook up a surprise
6. Use repetition

Use a Focus Object

The audience will probably be looking at you before you start speaking, so give them something to look at: a focus object that calls attention to you and the main point of your speech. Use an object or prop, a part or all of your clothing, a newspaper headline, a slide or chart or other visual, even another person to show the audience what you're going to tell them in the speech.

Example For a briefing on the development of a new product, the speaker is holding up two objects, one about the size of a pack of cigarettes, and the other the size of a book of matches:

"The objects I'm holding represent the difference between where we are and where we'd like to be on this project. The prototype of the (*name of device*) is functioning as it should be, but it's still too large. We can make it this big (hold up larger version), but we need to be able to make it this big (hold up smaller object). Really, we need to be able to make it this *small*."

Use Deliberate Silence

Here, *you* become the focus object. The audience wonders why you aren't speaking yet. Don't wait too long, or they'll stop wondering and you'll lose their attention. Don't look down at your notes, or they'll think you're just not ready yet.

Look at individuals in the audience and smile. If you're not going to relate the silence to the topic or purpose, just begin your speech. If you have a way to use the silence as an example of something in your speech, begin by explaining the meaning of the silence.

Example   For a presentation on improving corporate communications, there are ten seconds of silence as the speaker looks at the audience.

"What you just heard is what I hear when I ask the question, 'Should we have a meeting to develop a new plan?' Silence is the response. However, we all know what everybody's thinking—'Not another meeting!' "

Use an Anecdote, Story, or Fable

Notice that telling a joke is not included here. That's because comedians tell jokes. The purpose of the joke is to get a laugh. After the laugh (or no laugh), the comedian goes on to the next joke, one that is not necessarily related to the one before it or after it.

Speakers might want laughs also, but not for laughter's own sake. A speaker tells a story, humorous or otherwise, because the story illustrates an important point in the presentation. If the story is a funny one, that's a bonus.

Are you the type of person who can tell a joke well? If you are, you have an extra advantage. If you're not especially good at telling jokes, don't tell any. The price of getting off to a bad start is too high. Instead, tell a story that illustrates your point.

Example   This presentation is about the impact of a new set of statewide regulations.

"When Moses came down from the mountain with the Ten Commandments, he held up the two tablets to astonished onlookers and said, "These are *all* the rules. There are only ten. I carried these down by myself. You see how simple life will be? A single man can carry in his hands all the rules we have to live by.'

As the people started to return to their dwellings, marveling at the clarity and simplicity of the rules, Moses spoke again.

'By the way,' he said, 'I need one hundred strong men to go back up the mountain with me to carry down the regulations.' "

Use a Familiar Quotation

When we hear a bit of a familiar song, we may start thinking of the lyrics without even being aware of it. This reaction is the basis for using a familiar quotation: the audience starts to go along without consciously deciding to do so.

This method is particularly effective if you use the familiar quotation in an unusual way. Just when the listener thinks that he or she has anticipated where you're going, you change course a little for the effect of irony, humor, or contrast. You can change direction within the quotation, by changing a key word or words, or you can give the quotation and change its usual meaning.

Example   This is for a seminar on investment opportunities.

"To be a wise investor, you have to know enough to look before you leap. But you also have to know that he who hesitates is lost. How can you tell how long you should look before you leap? That's what we're going to find out."

Cook Up a Surprise

Surprises get people's attention, sometimes even shock them. There are many ways to cook up a surprise, but all are based on the same idea. First, you anticipate what the audience expects you to do. Then, you do something else. You could start with a short question or statement that is surprising enough to get people's attention, but not so strong as to be offensive.

You could start by stating the opposite of your point, and then showing why that thinking is wrong.

You can start by telling what you're *not* going to do. You can plant a question in your audience by using a confederate who will interrupt you at just the right moment with the question you want at that time.

Example   This is the introduction of a speaker, a technical consultant.

"Mr. Jackson's not here because we can't solve this problem. He's here because he's a specialist. We might see two of these problems each year, but he's seeing two every week. With our knowledge and his special experience, we're going to find the best and most efficient solution."

Use Repetition

Advertising and propaganda rely heavily on repetition to drive home the message. As a speaker, you must remember that the listening audience can't look back as a reader can. One use of repetition is as a reminder. Another is for emphasis. Repeating a word, a phrase, or a grammatical structure can focus audience attention. A simple way to do this is to start your first three or four sentences with the same few words. Also, try to keep the sentences in the same structure and at about the same length. Close off the repetition with a summary sentence that gives the main point of your speech.

Example   This example opens a keynote speech on alcoholism in industry.

"The alcoholic employee is an ineffective worker. The alcoholic employee is an unreliable family member. The alcoholic employee is an unproductive member of society. The alcoholic employee is everybody's problem."

HAVE THE LAST WORD: Finish Strong

Three crucial points have passed: the opening words, the overview, and the summary to lead into the conclusion. The last critical point approaches, the final words of your speech. You want to leave the audience with your main point. You might hope for thunderous applause, but you want, at the least, a graceful exit line. The audience should feel that your speech didn't just end, but that you *finished* it. Here are some effective closings that will help you to accomplish these purposes:

- Repeat and extend the opening
- Give a before-and-after picture
- Look to the future
- Offer a challenge

Repeat and Extend the Opening

This method has the added advantage of unifying your work by repeating the technique you used as an opener. As the listeners hear the closing, they will remember where they heard it before—in the opening words of the speech. You can use the focus object again, or use a new one related to the first one.

You can use deliberate silence again. You can retell the story and change the ending. You can add a new twist to the opening quotation or surprise. You can repeat the opening repetition after changing an element of it.

Example 1 For the alcoholism speech:

"With help provided by the program we've seen, the former alcoholic will no longer be everybody's problem, but will be a part of the solution. He or she can again be an effective worker, a reliable family member, and a productive member of society."

Example 2 Repeating the use of the focus object in the prototype briefing:

"Now we're *here* (hold up the larger object); in six weeks we want to be *here* (hold up the smaller object), or even *here* (hold up an even smaller object)."

Give a Before-and-After Picture

Contrast is an effective method of making your point. The closer together the things being contrasted, the sharper the contrast.

You might contrast the best possible outcome with the worst, an old method with a new, the past with the present, the present with the future. Be sure to finish with the view you're selling—the one you want to emphasize—because that is the one the audience is most likely to remember.

Example For a proposal to upgrade office equipment:

"The choice seems clear. We can continue to use our outdated equipment and require 30 minutes to put out a single business letter, or we can upgrade to word processing and complete the same work in less than half the time."

Look to the Future

Introductions tend to look to the past, to see how we got where we are. Conclusions tend to look to the future, to predict where we're going. To use this technique, decide what type of future you want the listener to consider: his or her individual future, the future of the company, the industry, the country, or the planet.

Example For a report on market trends:

"We can expect interest rates to rise again, but only gradually and not to the point of last year's high. We've seen fourteen record highs this year on the New York Exchange, and this is just the beginning. In the next few years, we're going to have to make bigger charts."

Offer a Challenge

What is the difference between a challenge and a dare? To say "I dare you to dive from the 10-meter platform" is not quite the same as saying "I challenge you to become the best you are capable of being." The difference is more than one of degree. If it is presented properly, a challenge makes the audience eager and proud to accept it, rather than afraid to turn it down. The way we're using it, *a challenge is a no-lose proposition.*

It is a call for action, and it asks the listener to do something to accomplish a goal, usually one in the listener's own interests. Offering a challenge in the last words focuses the entire speech on a single point: the action you want the listener to take.

Example □ For a commencement address:

"You are more than the hope of the future; you *are* the future. What you become is what the future will be. I challenge you, then, to become the best you are capable of being."

PUT IT ALL TOGETHER TO GET THE JOB DONE

Overviews, summaries, first words, last words—these are all techniques that will help you to accomplish your purpose as a speaker. To this point, most of our work has been in the planning and organizing of the written speech. We've been composing the lines for the actor to speak.

The next step is to look at the speaking situation and to see how the speech fits into the larger communication picture. In most business situations, the purpose of a presentation can be understood only by looking at this larger picture. The speaker needs to know:

- How many other presentations have been made, are being made, or will be made on this topic?

- What written materials have been used, are being used, or will be used to support this presentation?

- Should this report be spoken, written, or both?

The next chapter shows you the connections between speaking and writing in business reports, and helps you to answer the questions that will fit your presentation into the larger communication picture.

7

Say It or Write It?

"TECHNOLOGY TODAY IS POINTED TOWARD INCREASED TECHNICAL COMMUNICA-
tion, and innovations such as electronic mail, laser communications, and telecon-
ferencing are on the verge of becoming business practice. A few years from now
a briefer's presentation will be beamed via satellite to company audiences or to
audiences in other parts of the world."[1]

If the thought of speaking in front of a small group gives you stage fright,
imagine giving an oral briefing that is beamed to audiences all over the world!
Overcoming fear is not a matter of jumping into the water and either sinking or
swimming. Preparing and rehearsing build confidence, and confidence leads to
effective presentations, whether to one person or a worldwide audience.

GOOD SPEAKING STARTS WITH GOOD WRITING

One of the main points of this book is that effective *speaking* starts with effective
writing, based on careful analysis of audience and purpose, good organization,
and a convincing presentation of your main ideas with support or proof. There

---

[1]from "Oral Briefing versus Technical Report: Two Approaches to Communication Problems," by
William E. McCarron, in *Courses, Components, and Exercises in Technical Communication.* Copy-
right 1981 by the National Council of Teachers of English. Reprinted by permission of the pub-
lisher.

are other important connections between speaking and writing. Although there may be occasions when you can choose whether to make a spoken or a written presentation, there will be others in which one or the other will be called for. In many cases, you can use both forms—you can say it *and* write it—and have the advantages of both forms of communication.

Mr. William E. McCarron of the United States Air Force Academy is an experienced writer and briefer. He compares writing an oral briefing in these six areas:

- Graphics
- Delivery
- Organization
- Feedback
- Persuasion
- Compatibility

USE GRAPHICS OR VISUALS TO SHOW YOUR POINT

Good graphics can be to the oral briefing what a detailed outline is to the written report. The visual aid should contain the key points. In fact, when I am preparing a briefing, I keep two pads of paper in front of me; on one I write the text and on the other I sketch an *outline* (ideas for diagrams or tables) that will visually establish the points I intend to make.

If the audience does not always listen to what the briefer says, they nevertheless continue to see the important points on the screen in front of them.

A STRONG DELIVERY IS VITAL

A speaker's enthusiasm for the subject, voice modulation, and inflection enliven even the dullest subject. Conversely, even an interesting subject fails to attract listeners when it is delivered in a monotone. Writing is a different medium entirely. The author can control tone, the order of the subject matter, and the consistency of the report, but he or she cannot personally enliven the material. The ability of the briefer to speak with conviction and to interact with the audience and the visual aids is vital to the success of an oral briefing.

SELECT AND ORGANIZE YOUR DATA

A writer may blow an explanation or transition in a report, but the reader who has the leisure (or the patience) to sift out the important information will still garner the message. This is not the case in oral briefings. To omit a clear thesis statement or overview at the outset spells disaster for a speaker because the audience does not have the opportunity to skip ahead and pick up key points.

Selectivity is essential because the briefer lacks the luxury of time in front of an audience. Also, oral briefing is a slower process than silent reading.

Aside from the actual research or data gathering involved, the demand in industry today is for informal and formal briefings on the results of research and experiment. The greatest breakthroughs are ineffectual unless they are communicated to decision makers.

LOOK FOR AND REACT TO FEEDBACK

Feedback is a simple concept. It is the reaction of the reader or listener to what a person writes or says and the effect of that reaction on the writer or speaker. Feedback to technical writing is usually slow and deliberate; in an oral briefing, it is quick, often instantaneous. The oral briefer, even in the most formal presentation, is the recipient (or victim) of instant feedback.

Not only must the briefer react to direct feedback, but he or she must be sensitive to *indirect feedback:* a lifted eyebrow, a yawn, or a laugh.

The audience is not always a group of fellow professionals with a thorough knowledge of the material being presented. For a given briefing, the audience may initially be engineers, then middle managers in a corporation, then the city council who must vote on a technical proposal. An oral briefing can be as dynamic as the Dow-Jones Industrial Average. It can be modified or expanded to meet the needs of a variety of audiences.

PERSUADE THROUGH LOGIC AND INTEGRITY

Solid writing persuades readers to accept particular points about a subject. The same principle can be carried over to oral briefings. First, the briefer must select the arguments that best support key points. Second, the briefer must make those arguments convincing to a live audience in a limited amount of time. Finally, the success of the briefing often depends not so much on the quality of the arguments as on the integrity and stature of the briefer. In industry, it is the bank president who briefs the chamber of commerce on the dollars to be loaned for a new civic project.

The integrity of the briefer—the audience's belief that the briefer will not distort the subject matter—has traditionally been the strongest argument in public communication.

MAKE SPEAKING AND WRITING COMPATIBLE

Because technical briefings so often precede formal technical reports, one final point needs emphasis: compatibility. The oral briefing and the technical report must not contradict each other. If the conclusions of a final written report differ from the preliminary briefing, the writer must remind the readers precisely where the report differs from the briefing.

DO BOTH

When you can, enjoy the advantages of both writing and speaking by giving the audience a visual understanding of your main ideas. Be sure to keep the visual at the right level of detail: don't let the visuals replace you as a speaker. For example, listeners don't need your entire manuscript as a handout. If you give them too much to read in a glance, they'll either ignore the handout, or worse, ignore you, the speaker.

Use a handout or visual aid to provide a map of your destination and the route you'll take to get there.

The next chapter discusses Mr. McCarron's second criterion: delivery. Delivery and sensitivity to feedback can make or break any presentation, no matter how well planned it might be. Chapter 8 begins with advice from two professional speakers and listeners. The rest of the chapter shows you how to use their advice to make your delivery confident and professional.

8

Deliver It—The Other 90 Percent

SURELY—AFTER ANALYZING PURPOSE, AUDIENCE, AND SITUATION; AFTER USING A Pattern Guide to organize the presentation; after writing an opening, an overview, a summary, and a closing—the speaker must be nearly there, almost through. After all this, the speaker *is* almost there in terms of time—but has not yet begun to accomplish *the speaking purpose!* No words have been spoken yet, and the audience can't tell if the speaker is even going to show up on the right day.

Think of any spoken presentation as an audition for a part in a play. You can rehearse for ten weeks if you like, but you'll get the part or lose it on the day you actually audition. Many others will say the same lines you do on that day, but only one of you will be chosen for the part.

That's how important delivery is. It's the other 90 percent. Without the analyzing and planning and writing, no delivery could be possible, but your delivery is the part the audience actually sees and hears, so delivery determines whether you accomplish your purpose.

ESTABLISH YOURSELF AS SOMEONE WORTH LISTENING TO

Good delivery involves several things. You have to establish yourself as someone worth listening to. You have to keep things moving, keep the audience's interest. You have to keep contact—eye contact and brain contact—with the audience, and this means being adaptable enough to go to a fallback plan (or plans). You have to make the audience feel smart. You have to make them feel that you're giving them what they came for.

Let's turn to some professional listeners again for their thinking on coming on like a pro. The first listener is Ms. Helen Gurley Brown, the editor of *Cosmopolitan*. Her advice:

"I can only say the most important ingredient is not to *bore* anybody! This means not carrying on for one more sentence than is necessary to get the point across. It means cutting almost *any* presentation by several lines or slides or graphics, even if you think you've got it down to the bone. After that, I would suggest rehearse, rehearse, *rehearse* . . . you should come on like a total pro and that comes from being scared enough to get yourself up to your very peak performance with *practice*."

Conclusions

1. A professional gets *up* for a peak performance
2. Fear + Practice = Peak Performance

The next professional speaker and listener should be familiar from chapter 2. Ms. Nancy H. Roberts, former executive director of the Industry—Labor—Education Council, talks about using feedback to keep track of the audience's reaction.

Q: How can you tell when the audience is with you? How do you keep track of how you're doing?

A: I can tell by their reactions. If they're looking everywhere but at me, I know I've lost them and I have to get them back somehow. If they're sitting absolutely still, I know they're lost in space—not paying the slightest attention to the presentation.

If they're looking at me, they're listening to me, and I know I'm on track. If people ask questions, they were probably with me."

Q: How do you keep from losing them, and what do you do if it does happen?

A: Sometimes you make sure it doesn't happen by challenging the audience right at the beginning. It's usually an effective opening to ask: "Why are you here? What do you expect to find out at this presentation? What do you want?"

Of course, you have to be prepared for many possibilities if you start with pointed questions like these. You can't expect to ask these questions and then read a prepared speech word for word.

Keep it short, too. If I have a 40 to 45-minute speaking time, I try to keep my prepared remarks to about ten minutes—no more than twenty. I think that's about as long as anyone can listen with full concentration. I usually tell the audience at the beginning that I'm going to open things up to questions after the first ten minutes, and that lets them know they're going to get a chance to ask about what's personally important to them.

Anything that gets the audience to focus on *you* and on the *topic* right away will make an effective opening. Sometimes I take a quick survey of the audience to see what their interests are before I begin. If I know my topic well enough, I should be able to tailor my presentation to fit the personal needs expressed in my quick survey.

Q: How can you conduct a survey in such a short time?

A: If the group isn't too large, I give people cards and ask them to write a question or an area of interest. If my presentation is supposed to cover four main topics, for example, I might ask people to rank the topics. When I collect the cards, I can quickly see how much time and emphasis to give each topic.

It's a good idea to listen to the person who introduces you, also. You might find the key to the audience in what happens before you make your presentation.

One of my first presentations was at a dinner meeting of a men's group. Part of the business conducted at the meeting (before my speech) was a report on a survey taken to see what kinds of topics and speakers the men wanted at their dinner meetings. The number one topic was sports. I don't think my topic (cooperation between industry and education) even made the list. Right after the results were reported, I was introduced.

I stood up and said, 'The survey shows that you couldn't care less about my topic, so I'm tearing up my speech.' And I did. I tore it in two and threw it away.

'You've said you're interested in sports, so I'm going to tell you a sports story. Did you ever hear of (and I named a big-time college football player)? Of course you have. I want to tell you about the time I beat him at leg wrestling at a college fraternity party.'

When I finished the story, I told them I had to go back to my main topic and tell them a little bit about that, also. This example is a little extreme, but it shows that you have to *make contact with the audience that is out there,* not the one you hoped was going to be there.

You've got to get some interaction. Since most of my presentations are made to people in the manufacturing industry, I usually carry safety glasses and a hard hat around with me. I'm not really trying to be one of the boys, but the props give me a light way to get started. From there I go directly to what I *do* know about their business or industry, and that helps to establish me as somebody worth listening to.''

Conclusions

1. Your delivery has to get and keep the audience's attention.
2. Your delivery has to establish you as somebody worth listening to.
3. Your fallback plan may allow you to return to your primary plan.

The rest of this chapter shows you how to come on like a total pro, somebody worth listening to, by using the speaker's advantages.

GET THE SPEAKER'S ADVANTAGES

Chapter 3 explains that meaning is conveyed by all of these:

1. The physical setting
2. Dress or attire
3. Posture, gesture, and other body language
4. Facial expression and eye contact
5. Tone, inflection, and loudness
6. The words themselves

Earlier chapters deal with advantage number six, preparing the script. With good planning, you'll get that advantage. This chapter shows how to get the other five.

Leo Rosten explains ''How to Tell a Joke'' in an article in *50 Plus* magazine (June, 1985). His rules apply to giving a speech, also:

1. Tell it at a brisk pace.
2. Take a direct route to the climax.
3. End with a clear, exact punch line.

He extends these ideas with a few more tips:

1. Include only those characters who are essential to the point.
2. Show that you're enjoying yourself—smile.
3. Keep eye contact with your listeners—look from face to face.
4. Use simple language.
5. Plan for the exact wording and rhythm of the punch line.

This list looks very much like a list of requirements for delivering the perfect speech. Let's look at the speaker's advantages, one at a time, to see how you can have all six going for you when you make your next presentation.

Scout Out the Physical Setting

If you have anything to say about the physical setting for your presentation, organize it to suit your audience and purpose. If you want an informal atmosphere, keep the audience close to you. Don't speak from a raised platform. If the audience is close to you physically, they'll feel close in other ways, also. It will be easy for you to keep eye contact, and you probably won't need to use a microphone, which means you'll be able to speak more naturally.

If you want a more formal tone, keep the audience at more of a distance and speak from a raised platform.

In many cases, the physical setting will not be a matter of choice for you. Even so, you can still use the setting to your advantage. Like a good commander seeking the high ground, you can choose a vantage point in almost any setting.

Start by making yourself familiar with the surroundings. This will allow you to feel and to look comfortable in the setting, as if you belong there. Also, by knowing the *flavor* of the setting—from formal to informal, spare to busy—you can be sure to dress so as to look right in that setting. If you look and feel right, you will have advantage number one.

Dress for Success

Your clothing will say something about you, and unless you're hiding backstage, your clothing is sure to speak before you do. Color and style will make an impression on the audience.

Even though your presentation may not have the status of a royal visit, your appearance is important because it influences the audience's reactions. Your appearance is part of what they come to know of you during the presentation. Decide what impression you want to make, and then dress accordingly. If you're presenting yourself as an authority, you can help yourself by dressing the part. You can still do something surprising—put on your hard hat, if you wish—but make the first impression count for you. If you dress appropriately, you've got advantage number two.

Move with Confidence

Let's say you've prepared the speech and checked out the setting. You've dressed to set the right tone and to look as if you belong in the setting. Before you speak and as you speak, your body will be speaking, too. *How* you move and *how much* you move will make an impression on your audience.

Your posture can help you to communicate your message. Stand straight but relaxed, with your weight on both feet, and you'll look confident and at ease. Gesture normally, and you'll look as if you are one person talking to another, instead of an impersonal orator addressing impersonal multitudes.

In order to move naturally, you have to keep your hands free. Don't hold a cigarette, a pipe, or anything else that could get in your way or restrict your hand movements. When your hands are tied up, the rest of your body won't move much, either, and you could look frozen in place. It's not easy to pay attention to talking statues, so allow yourself to move. The more you move, and the more naturally you move, the faster you and your audience will warm up.

Be sure to use speaking notes that allow you freedom of movement. Reading from a script makes movement nearly impossible. If you can move at all, your gestures will look like mechanical interludes in a robot-like reading.

Use a Pattern Guide (explained in chapter 6) to develop an outline for speaking notes, and you will free yourself from the text. Then you'll have advantage number three.

Keep Contact with Your Audience

How do you feel when you're talking with someone and that person isn't smiling and won't look you in the eye? It's hard to be responsive to such a speaker.

Make yourself easy to respond to my smiling and keeping eye contact. Besides warming up the audience, smiling warms you up. Smiling will help you to look relaxed and to feel relaxed.

Eye contact is just as important. If you use efficient speaking notes or a Pattern Guide, you can look at your audience. Scanning back and forth like a security camera, however, is not the way to do this. You don't want the audience to feel as if they're being watched; you want them to feel as if you're talking to them.

Make eye contact by looking directly at individuals as you are speaking. As you go through your presentation, select people in different areas of the audience and meet their eyes for a few seconds. This is easier to do in smaller groups, but it's necessary when speaking to a group of any size. By looking directly into the camera and by being free of the notes, a television news reporter can make each person in a viewing audience of millions feel in personal contact. In fact, one factor in hiring television personalities is their ability to convey this feeling of personal communication to a viewing audience.

When you are speaking, it is all too easy to think that *you* are the most important person in the room, or to think that your speech is the foremost thing on everyone's minds. *No one in your audience will share either of these feelings.* Think of yourself as the quarterback, and think of your speech as the football. If no one on your team can catch it, then it doesn't matter how high or how far you throw it—the result will be the same: no gain. Even if you're not ready to be the chief television reporter for NBC news, you can remember that your ratings determine your effectiveness (and your salary). Smile and look at people as you talk to them, and you'll have advantage number four.

Use Your Voice Effectively

So far, we're still working on a silent movie. Tone, inflection, and loudness— these and other factors of oral presentation will be great determiners of the effectiveness of your speech.

Let's start with *pace*, the speed at which you deliver the words. Although it is our habit to speak more slowly in order to be understood better, studies show that slower isn't always clearer or better. On listening comprehension tests, speeded-up tapes produced better comprehension scores than tapes at normal speed. (Making a compressed-speech tape is not a simple procedure, however; it can't be done by simply running the tape through faster, which produces a "chipmunk" effect as sound is distorted.)

Word-per-minute speed is relative. A good typist might type accurately at 60 words per minute. A practiced speaker might speak at 150 words per minute. An efficient reader might read 1000 words per minute. But these are all slow speeds to the brain, which can work at much higher speeds than these. The point is not to race the audience to the finish line, but to deliver the speech in a crisp manner. Slow down for emphasis and variety, but set a fairly rapid pace if you want to keep the audience in touch with your thoughts. Unless someone has a meter running, clock time is less important than *psychological* time. Psychological time is the *apparent* passing of time, and it can fly or drag, depending on how much fun you're having.

People's time is important to them, so you must make them feel that you're making good use of it. Since the audience is always right, this perception is more important than the reality of your pace. Keep the pace up, and it will seem that you're moving quickly and getting a lot done in a short time. Vary the pace to make your speech more interesting. A further advantage of varying the pace is that it helps you to vary the volume and pitch of your delivery.

Volume or *loudness* affects other qualities of voice. Unless you are a very practiced speaker, trying to speak loudly causes your voice to tighten up. The *tone* changes and you will sound shrill or harsh and tense. It is important to look, sound, and feel relaxed, so don't force your voice. If you're looking at people in your audience, you'll be able to tell immediately by their reaction if your volume is okay.

Inflection is related to volume. Inflection normally rises at the end of a question and falls at the end of a statement. Be careful that you don't let it fall out of hearing range. Keep the volume up at the ends of sentences, and your audience will be able to hear you.

Variations in loudness, tone, inflection, or anything else can be used to create emphasis. *Silence,* too, can help you to make your point. A pause serves as a kind of oral punctuation, and a few seconds of deliberate silence can be more effective than a shout. Deliberate silence is a signal that something important is coming up. Be sure to look at the audience, however, so that they don't misinterpret the silence. You don't want them to think you've lost your place or are trying to catch your breath.

Keep things moving at a crisp pace, keep your voice relaxed, use variety for emphasis, and you'll have advantage number five.

Rehearse for Peak Performance

Almost all of these factors of delivery hinge on one crucial point: *practice.* You must know your presentation well enough to be free from your notes. You must be free to move and gesture normally, free to look at people in your audience, free to move at a crisp pace, free to pay attention to what you're doing and to make any changes required to accomplish your purpose.

Using a Pattern Guide for your notes can get you this freedom. You can probably put the whole presentation on one sheet of paper. If your presentation is especially long, stretch out a Pattern Guide to two pages. Don't try to write complete sentences, but do include the first and last words.

As explained in chapter 6, the Guide is an outline of your main points. Number the details that go with each main point. This makes them easier to spot. Type or print your notes, and mark any points of special emphasis.

Make sure you can use your notes in the actual setting—at the distance from which you'll be looking at them. Practice using them at this distance, and practice *aloud*. Whizzing through your speech at a subvocal mutter gives you neither the sense nor the flavor of the words. If you're going to use a microphone, practice with it to get used to the sound of your amplified voice. If you're going to be first at the mike, the urge to test it may be strong. If you want to look like a pro, resist the urge. Don't tap or blow on the mike. Don't say "Testing . . ." or "Is this thing on?" Just start your speech with something short enough for you to tell if the mike is working properly. Look at the audience and you'll know if you're being heard.

Prepare a Pattern Guide for your fallback plan also, but keep it out of the way until you know you'll need it.

Here are some sample notes for the first part (the Problem) of a presentation from a department head to the employees in his department. The purpose of this Level-Three (Problem-Solution) presentation is to offer a plan to make meetings more productive.

Problem   (10-sec. pause . . . and look at them)
Did you hear that? That's what I hear when I ask "Should we have a meeting to develop a new plan?" Silence. But we all know what everybody's thinking: "Not another meeting!"

1. Nobody wants meetings . . . seen as necessary evil, last mtg. example
2. Few contribute . . . absence, lateness, boredom, newspapers
3. Attitude gets little accomplished . . . need 3 to do job of 1
4. *Yet meetings are important tools for us—we can't do business without them!*

A complete Pattern Guide in this form could serve as notes for a presentation of 15-20 minutes. The notes would fit on a single page, and the speaker could be free to move and gesture, to look at the audience, to pay attention to his or her own performance, and to make changes required to better accomplish the purpose.

In the next chapter, you will see how to use Planning Guides to help you to develop, rehearse, and deliver your presentations in the business speaking situations that count.

9

Manage Your Future

THERE'S A BONUS TO DEVELOPING YOUR SPEAKING SKILLS. IF YOU ENCOUNTER just one important business speaking situation each day, you'll have over 200 opportunities each year to use your new techniques to get what you want. Most of these opportunities will come with the people with whom you spend a large share of your waking hours: the people with whom you work.

Unless you're at one of the extremes of the corporate structure, you have superiors, peers, and subordinates. Some report to you; others, you report to. Most of the speech interaction in your job may involve just these few people, so it is in your interest to speak wisely and well to them.

In 1982 a book came along that brought management theory into the realm of pop culture. *The One-Minute Manager* [1] tells how a manager can get efficient results from subordinates through setting one-minute goals and giving one-minute praisings and reprimands.

Although the book often mentions honesty and directness, some readers apparently felt that the techniques were more manipulative than honest or direct. Two of these readers, Rae Andre and Peter D. Ward, wrote a response called *The 59-Second Employee.* [2] This book's point is simple: the One-Minute

---

[1] Kenneth Blanchard and Spencer Johnson, *The One-Minute Manager* (New York: William Morrow & Co., 1982).

[2] Rae Andre and Peter D. Ward, *The 59-Second Employee* (Boston: Houghton Mifflin, 1984).

Manager is out to manipulate you, so use the techniques in our book to manage *upward*—to manage the manager by staying one second ahead. Each book ends with a game plan.

The One-Minute Manager's game plan is to, *"Set goals, praise and repri-mand behaviors, encourage people, speak the truth, laugh, work, enjoy* and encourage the people you work with to do the same as you do." (p. 101)

The 59-Second Employee's Game Plan is to:

"Go to work on it.

Get more information.

Learn.

(And learn how to learn.)

About your company

About your boss.

About yourself.

Manage up.

Fix it if you can.

Move on if you want.

Live with it if you must.

But definitely . . .

Apply the Law of the Tanobway (There ain't no one best way!)" (p. 92)

Whether you're on one of these sides, on both, or somewhere in the mid-dle, you need to cope with the personal styles of the people with whom you work. Both books imply that the pretense of honesty is as close to honesty as you're going to get, but it might be possible to use some of the techniques we've discussed in this book to effect a friendly merger between these two attitudes.

If we can get rid of the psyching and counterpsyching we are left with a few simple techniques to help people work together for their mutual benefit. The features that are important in a formal speaking situation are just as important in day-to-day business speaking.

These Principles

- Speaking is a transaction
- Find out what you're hired to do
- Know the audience's needs
- Define your purpose clearly
- To get what *you* want, give the audience what *they* want

- Be complete, brief, focused, and organized

- Speak in a direct, personal way
- Have a plan and a fallback plan

Lead to these Suggestions

- Let's set goals together: we're more likely to work together to accomplish *our* goals than to accomplish yours or mine.
- Let's define good and not-so-good performance at least three times: *before* we start, *as* we work, and *after* we've finished.
- Let's find a way to get what *we* want, because there ''ain't no one best way''!

10

Plan for Success—
The Speaker's
Planning Guide

THIS IS THE CHAPTER THAT SHOWS YOU HOW TO GO TO WORK. THERE ARE PLANning Guides in Part II for each speaking situation discussed. Each guide includes all you need to prepare for the speaking situation—from planning to final evaluation:

- An explanation of the usual situation, including place, occasion, and audience

- An analysis of the speaker's purpose

- An explanation of typical mistakes made in this situation—and how to avoid them

- The steps to success for planning your presentation

- An Audience Inventory to help you to pinpoint your audience's information needs

- A Pattern Guide to organize your work

- A Special Tactics sheet to plan for the critical spots in your presentation
- An Evaluation Checklist to help you to decide if you've got the perfect speech—*before* you give it—and to help you revise it if you don't

The guides in Part II are grouped according to whether they are one-way or two-way speaking situations. Chapters 11 through 15 discuss such one-way situations as:

- Introducing a speaker
- Giving a lecture or address
- Making a proposal/giving a solution strategy
- Making a demonstration/giving directions
- Giving a report or briefing

Chapters 16 through 19 discuss the following two-way situations:

- Working in a discussion group or panel
- Brainstorming/problem-solving
- Interviewing/making a telephone presentation
- Debating/arguing a case/negotiating

Chapters 11 through 19 contain Planning Guides for each of these situations. Each guide is designed to be self-contained. After you find the guide for the presentation you are planning, start by reading about the speaking situation, the purpose, and the mistakes to avoid. With these in mind, continue by reading the steps to success. You can make notes on the Audience Inventory and the Pattern Guide.

Some of the speaking situations are so open-ended that only your specific circumstances can dictate the pattern to be used. In these cases, I provide Pattern Guides, Audience Inventories, Special Tactics sheets, and Evaluation Checklists for different circumstances.

SPECIAL CONSIDERATIONS IN TWO-WAY SITUATIONS

Because discussion is a team sport, there are additional sections in chapters 16 and 17 which deal with the performance of the group as a whole. Under the usual mistakes, there is a section called "Loss of Balance" which shows typical reasons for unproductive group performance. Under the steps to success, there is a section called "Direct the Group." This section shows how you can keep the group focused and productive by supplying what is needed at critical points in the discussion.

The Planning Guide for chapter 19 has sections called ''The Means to the Ends,'' which contain categories for strategy and tactics of negotiation.

Before using the Planning Guides for two-way situations, review chapter 5 for another look at the explanations of initiating, clarifying, and reacting behaviors.

POLISHING YOUR PRESENTATION

When you've done the research and writing necessary to complete the Audience Inventory and the Pattern Guide, use the Special Tactics sheet to make sure you've prepared for crucial spots in the speech. Then use the Evaluation Checklist to see if you have the perfect speech. After you've made revisions and improvements, use another Pattern Guide for your speaking notes. Notes in pattern form will be easy for you to follow, and the Guide will contain enough information for a well-planned and well-rehearsed presentation.

The rest of this chapter shows how the parts of a Speaker's Planning Guide are used to prepare a presentation. In this example, the speaker is a mid-level manager who is asked to study a problem and propose a solution. After completing the research, the speaker will prepare the presentation by using the Audience Inventory, Pattern Guide, Special Tactics sheet, and Evaluation Checklist.

THE SPEAKER'S PLANNING GUIDE: Making a Proposal/Giving a Solution Strategy

The Speaking Situation

One-way

The Place

Larry's office (Larry is the department head requesting the proposal.)

The Occasion

Recommending a course of action

The Audience

Larry

The Speaker's Purpose

To sell a plan of action by showing *why* and *how* a thing should be done.

THE AUDIENCE INVENTORY

Type of Presentation   Short briefing on a solution strategy

Size and Makeup of Audience   Larry and Larry's immediate supervisor

1. Who are these people? What is their background in this business or technical area?
   Larry has been aware of the absenteeism problem since he took over as department head four years ago.

2. What is their experience in this area?
   He's seen other solutions tried and seen their lack of success. He's never offered a solution upstairs (to his supervisor) on such a big problem.

3. What are their special interests? What do they want from me?
   He'd like a chance for a real success with his supervisor—top management—as well as a more efficient department.

4. What are my purposes? What do I want to give them?
   I want to give him a job done well, so he'll remember who got this job done when it comes time to pick the next department head.

5. How can I match up these wants lists?
   If I accomplish his purpose, I'll accomplish mine.

***

6. What do they know about the company (or other group) I represent?
   He knows that money-saving ideas get rewarded from above.

7. What do they know about my background, experience, and professional reputation?
   Larry knows I came up with the solution to the problem with the printers.

***

8. How are they likely to react to my ideas on this issue or proposal? Will they be likely to agree? To what extent?
   If he sees that it works, he'll take it upstairs.

9. What kinds of evidence would be most convincing to them?
   First common sense, and then dollars and cents. He'll want the ideas and then the numbers.

10. What level of detail should be included?
    At this point, only the big picture, general ideas.

***

11. How are they accustomed to getting information?
    How long will they want to listen?
    He'll want to see the picture in two or three minutes, since this is a preliminary report at this stage.

12. How would they want the material organized? Where would they want me to begin?
    He'll want to get to the solution quickly, so I'll state the problem briefly.

***

13. What do they have to be able to do on the basis of the information and arguments I present?
    Put in practice a solution to a good-sized problem, employee absenteeism.

14. Should they be aware of a trend? Able to draw a conclusion? Able to make a decision?
    He's got to decide whether to take this upstairs, and they'll have to decide whether to go companywide with the solution.

***

15. What questions will they be likely to ask?
    He'll eventually want to know how much it would cost, how much it might save, and how long it would take us to get it started. He'll want to know if this has worked anywhere else.
    If he likes the idea, the first think he'll want to know is how long it will take me to do a full report.

PATTERN GUIDE: Problem-Solution—Level Three

Problem

Employee absenteeism is increasing, with most of the absences falling on Monday and Friday.

Effects

We're sliding down to a three-day work week. On a Monday or a Friday we are always missing at least one person we need. This is interrupting work because most of our large-scale projects require contributions from everybody before decisions can be made.

Causes

Weekends are getting extended in both directions as people use their fifteen days of paid sick leave as vacation time to make three-day weekends.

Solution

If we try to restrict or verify sick-leave use, we're getting into the detective business, and we're probably asking for trouble by making a rule we can't enforce. Since people respond better to rewards than to punishments, let's reward people for *not* using sick leave—pay them $50 a day for unused sick leave, either at the end of the year or on the basis of what they've accumulated by retirement. This is like the phone company giving customers credit for not making information calls. If you make them, you lose the credit you would have earned.

Significance

By getting employees to work more regularly, we'll function more effectively and save money in the long run.

SPECIAL TACTICS FOR CRUCIAL POINTS

I will show them my plan and keep them on track by:

    __X__ Giving an Overview
    _____ Using a Printed Handout
    _____ Using a Graphic or Visual

Notes and Text for tactic chosen   In the first minute I'll suggest we create an attendance incentive to bring people to work five days a week.

I will create focus with the first words by:

    _____   Using a Focus Object
    _____   Using Deliberate Silence
    _____   Using an Anecdote, Fable, or Story
    _____   Using a Famous Quotation
    __X__   Cooking Up a Surprise
    _____   Using Repetition

Notes and Text for Tactic Chosen   The surprise will be a twist. Instead of suggesting a punishment or rigid enforcement, I'll suggest a system of rewards: "Some people are abusing the system, so I propose we reward them so they'll stop."

I will finish strong with the last words by:

    _____   Repeating and Extending the Opening
    __X__   Giving a Before-and-After Picture
    _____   Looking to the Future
    _____   Offering a Challenge

Notes and Text for Tactic Chosen   Right now we're paying people for five days of work, even though some of them are showing up for only three or four. If the new program will provide enough incentive to get them here all five days, we'll have a smooth-running department and we'll probably save more money than it will cost us for the incentives.

EVALUATION CHECKLIST: Problem-Solution—Level Three

The Situation

    YES   Did you find out exactly what you're hired to do?
    YES   Do you know the significance of the occasion?
    YES   Did you use the Inventory to find the audience's information needs?
    YES   Do you know your purpose—exactly what you want from this audience?
    YES   Do you know the actual physical setting of your presentation?

Revising Plan for Situation

Problem

YES   Does your opening focus the audience's attention on your main idea?

YES   Have you given an overview which shows your destination and route?

NO   Have you clearly shown the limits of the problem—how big, how much, how many, how long—in terms your audience can understand?

Revising Plan for Problem: Give the big numbers here: total number of absentees, number on Monday and Friday, estimated annual loss of revenue from absenteeism.

Effects

YES   Have you illustrated the most dramatic or important effects?

YES   Have you focused on a few effects instead of trying to list dozens?

YES   Have you shown your audience how *they* will be affected?

Revising Plan for Effects

Causes

YES   Have you given the most important cause or causes? Did you need to rule out other causes to isolate the ones you've identified?

NO   Have you given sufficient evidence to establish these causes?

YES   Have you directly related the causes to the problem and effects?

Revising Plan for Causes   Mention other causes. If alcoholism, for example, is another possible cause, we might be able to tell by seeing who this program doesn't reach.

Solution

YES   Is your solution strategy clear and specific?

YES   Have you given enough detail to show how the solution will work?

YES   Have you told the audience what you want them to think or to do?

YES   Have you linked the solution to the causes? To the significance?

YES   Have you given a summary of your main points so far?

Revising Plan for Solution

Significance

YES   Have you shown all of the benefits of your solution? The long-range benefits as well as the short-range or immediate ones?

YES   Have you identified what individuals and groups will benefit?

YES   Do your final words really *finish* the presentation? This is your last chance with the audience. Have you made an effective closing?

Revising Plan for Significance

Delivery

YES   Have you prepared speaking notes for the actual physical setting?

YES   Have you written out the first sentence and the last sentence?

YES   Have you rehearsed *aloud* with your notes in the actual setting?

YES   Have you rehearsed with a microphone, lectern, overhead projector, props, and every other piece of equipment you'll use?

YES   Have you planned your attire to set the tone for the situation and purpose?

NO   Have you prepared and rehearsed a fallback plan?

Revising Plan for Delivery   In addition to my notes, I should have ready a one-page pattern outline of my presentation. Then if we're interrupted, I can leave it with him. Even if we're not interrupted, I can leave the outline with him if he likes the plan.

LOOKING AHEAD

Now you're ready to go on to Part II and plan and write the presentations that will get you what you want.

Part II
Speaker's Planning Guides

11

Introducing a Speaker

The Speaking Situation

One-way

The Place

Lecture hall, auditorium, banquet room, or a smaller setting.

The Occasion

Meetings, awards ceremonies, commencements, anniversaries, and other significant events.

The Audience

From a few to a few thousand, but usually between 50 and 500.

The Speaker's Purpose

To show how the background, experience, and position of the person you're introducing relates to the audience and occasion. In essence, you're presenting the speaker's credentials as they relate to *this* audience.

The Planning Guides

For this situation, you will need the Statement-Support group of forms.

THE USUAL MISTAKES

Audience

Giving the speaker's name, but not his or her credentials. The job is to introduce, not announce, the person who will be speaking.

Purpose and Occasion

Introducing the wrong speaker or the wrong speech. There's probably no faster way to make oneself appear completely incompetent, and to get the speaker off to a horrible start.

Saying "This speaker needs no introduction." There's no good move after that. Following this statement with an introduction makes you look foolish, and following it with *no* introduction is just as bad.

Information Needs

Giving away the speaker's entire speech. You're supposed to prepare the audience for the main speaker, not make the main speaker unnecessary.

Focus and Organization

Falling in love with the microphone. Don't talk about yourself for ten minutes. Don't tell a joke or story that has nothing to do with the speaker or the situation.

Trying to tell *everything* the speaker has done during the past fifteen years, even though 95 percent of these accomplishments are not relevant to this speaking situation and audience. If we're told that the keynote speaker has adopted twelve children, climbed Mount Everest, and bicycled across Peru, we should also be told what this has to do with the situation.

Delivery

Speaking too fast, slowly, loudly, or softly.

Relying too much or not enough on notes. The speaker who tries to "wing it" is often shot down, and the one who reads the introduction into the microphone puts the audience to sleep.

THE STEPS TO SUCCESS

Make it relevant to your audience

Make sure you understand the significance of the occasion to the audience. Use the Audience Inventory to try to understand the information needs of the main speaker's audience. You'll need to know, for example, how much they already know about the speaker.

Make it complete and documented

Get the speaker's name right, and make sure you can pronounce it correctly. Write it out phonetically if you have to.

Make sure you know who the speaker is representing for this specific presentation. Further, make sure you know what the speaker has been hired to do, so that you can present him or her in the right context.

Do the research. Find out enough about the speaker to be able to select pertinent examples from background and experience. You may tell only 5 percent of what you found out about the speaker, but it should be the right 5 percent.

Make it brief and focused

Keep it down to a minute or two. Avoid "I remember when . . ." stories. These usually turn out to be more about the introducer than about the speaker. Give your own name and position, and then don't talk about yourself again. If you plan for two minutes, you will have about three hundred words to use.

Make it organized

Use the Statement-Support pattern to organize your introduction. The speaker will have to make his or her own case with the audience; your job is to give the speaker the best chance to do so. Three well-chosen supports will be more effective than an endless list of details.

Use Statement-Support to organize the fallback plan, also.

Make it interesting, easy to follow, and polished

Plan your notes in pattern form, and at the right level of detail to suit your memory and speaking style. Do this for the primary plan and the fallback plan.

Rehearse, rehearse, *rehearse*. Practice with your notes in the *actual physical setting:* standing at a podium, sitting at a table, etc.

Practice with a microphone and any other props or equipment you'll actually use.

Practice the primary plan and the fallback plan.

Leave your hands free to gesture normally.

12

Giving a
Lecture or Address

The Speaking Situation

One-way

The Place

Lecture hall, auditorium, banquet room, or a smaller setting.

The Occasion

Meetings, awards ceremonies, commencements, anniversaries, and other significant events.

The Audience

From a few to a few thousand, but usually between 50 and 500.

The Speaker's Purpose

The purpose will vary with the audience and the occasion, but the purpose is generally to inform and entertain. A commencement speaker, for example, will congratulate and try to inspire the graduating class, while an after-dinner speaker might try to entertain with amusing stories. A speaker at a conference might inform the audience about the latest trends in industry, or warn them of a worsening problem.

The Planning Guides

For this situation, you will need the Statement-Support, Thesis-Proof, Opinion-Reason, and Problem-Solution groups of forms.

THE USUAL MISTAKES

Audience

Missing the audience. Talking above or below the audience makes the speaker ineffective. This mistake is caused by the speaker's failure to understand the background, experience, and present information needs of the audience.

Purpose and Occasion

Doing the wrong job. Our professional listeners have told us that the speaker's chief concern should be to do the job he or she was hired to do. Part of the speaker's responsibility is to find out what that job is. This will require asking questions. If the audience is expecting an analysis of economic indicators, the speaker had better not launch into a repertoire of funny stories.

Information Needs

Giving incomplete information. It is frustrating to get the promise of the right information, but then not to get it all. This is like giving someone five digits of a telephone number—they're useless without the last two.

Offering no evidence or documentation. An intelligent audience will want to know where the speaker's conclusions come from. Even on matters of opinion, all opinions aren't equal. The speaker should show the foundation of fact and experience upon which the opinions are based.

Talking too long, and then leaving no time for questions. Think of the speeches and presentations you've listened to. In how many cases did you wish the speaker had talked longer?

Focus and Organization

Focusing on nothing in particular. This mistake is usually caused by poor planning and organizing. The speaker rambles on, filling the allotted time, but accomplishing no goal that the audience can detect. This mistake is compounded when the speech's introduction doesn't outline what the rest of the speech will cover. When a speaker doesn't make clear the "destination," it might be that there is none.

Saying "something must be done" and then not telling what it is that should be done. This mistake is common in persuasive speeches because it is so much easier to talk about problems than it is to talk about solutions. The something-must-be-done speech fits the Problem-*No*-Solution pattern, and it's not much help to the audience. Hearing such a speech is a little like going to your doctor and listening to a long list of your ailments, including all the future projections of more serious developments. As you sit there waiting for the prescription of some restorative treatment, the doctor looks down and says, "Something must be done. Thank you. Next patient."

Delivery

Speaking too fast, slowly, loudly, or softly.

Relying too much or not enough on notes. Relying too little can cause the speaker to lose contact with the speech: relying too much can cause the speaker to lose contact with the audience.

THE STEPS TO SUCCESS

Make it relevant to your audience

Understand the audience's background and experience. Use the Audience Inventory to try to pinpoint their information needs.

Find out exactly what you're hired to do on the occasion. Whoever asks you to speak should be able to answer your questions about the audience, occasion, and purpose. Find out what level of speaking is required (Level One, Two, or Three) and plan accordingly.

Talk for a reasonable length of time—perhaps 15-20 minutes—and then allow for questions. You might tell the audience at the beginning of your presentation that you'll leave time for questions at the end. If there is a question you *want* asked, plant it in the audience. It will serve as an ice-breaker, as the first question almost always prompts three or four more.

Make it complete and documented

Give complete information and document your conclusions. This isn't name-dropping; it's establishing credibility by showing your selection of sources. Give enough information for the audience to understand the basis of your view.

In a Level-Three situation, go deeper. The audience will need enough information on which to base a decision.

Make it brief and focused

Focus directly on the topic and make the focus clear from the start. Let an overview show your destination and the route you plan to take to get the audience there.

Make it organized

Plan your speech with an appropriate pattern. For Level One, use Statement-Support. For Level Two, use Thesis-Proof. For Level Three, use Problem-Solution or Opinion-Reason.

Organize both primary and fallback plans with the same pattern.

Make it interesting, easy to follow, and polished

Plan your notes (for *both* plans) in pattern form, and at the right level of detail to suit your memory and your speaking style.

Rehearse, rehearse, *rehearse*. Practice with your notes in the *actual physical setting:* standing at a podium, sitting at a table, etc. Practice with a microphone and with any other props or equipment you'll use in the presentation.

Practice the primary plan and the fallback plan.

Leave your hands free to gesture normally.

13

Making a Proposal/ Giving a Solution Strategy

The Speaking Situation

One-way

The Place

Office, boardroom, or meeting room.

The Occasion

Bidding on a project, recommending a course of action.

The Audience

Other firms or clients, management at various levels (usually superiors and decision-makers)

The Speaker's Purpose

To sell a plan of action by showing *why* and *how* a thing should be done.

The Planning Guides

For this situation, you will need the Opinion-Reason and Problem-Solution groups of forms.

THE USUAL MISTAKES

Audience

Becoming (unasked) an industrial philosopher and discussing abstract and unmeasurable goals ("We'll all feel better about ourselves.")

Failing to consider what evidence will be convincing to this audience.

Purpose and Occasion

Forgetting to *sell the solution*. It's easier to talk about problems, so speakers often do. Sell the solution.

Information Needs

Burying decision-makers in details they don't need or don't want.

Failing to offer alternatives and to show why they won't work as well as the solution you're offering.

Focus and Organization

Failing to relate the *why* to the *how*.

Springing the solution on the audience in the last thirty seconds, without giving them time or reason to believe in it.

Delivery

Speaking too fast, slowly, loudly, or softly.

Relying too much or too little on notes.

THE STEPS TO SUCCESS

Make it relevant to your audience

Use the Audience Inventory to develop types of evidence that will be persuasive to this audience.

Know the importance of the proposal and, if possible, the prevailing views toward it. Know which members of the audience you really have to sell, and aim the presentation at them.

Make it complete and documented

Show the solution or action you want in detail. Quickly show why other alternatives are not as good.

Give sources of your data and tell how current your information is.

Have detailed documentation ready if anyone asks for it.

Make it brief and focused

Make it 10 percent problem and 90 percent solution or recommendation.

Keep it down to ten or fifteen minutes, and tell the audience you'll leave time for questions at the end.

Make it organized

Use the Problem-Solution or Opinion-Reason pattern to organize both your primary plan and your fallback plan.

Use a visual to *show* what you'll tell. Give a one-page overview (in pattern form) before the presentation, and provide extra copies at the presentation.

Make it interesting, easy to follow, and polished

Plan your notes in pattern form, and at the right level of detail to suit your memory and speaking style.

Rehearse, rehearse, *rehearse*. Practice with your notes in the *actual physical setting:* standing at a podium, sitting at a table, etc. Practice with a microphone and any other props or equipment you'll actually use.

Practice the primary plan and the fallback plan.

Leave your hands free to gesture normally.

14

Making a Demonstration/ Giving Directions

The Speaking Situation

One-way

The Place

Meeting room, lecture hall.

The Occasion

Development of a new product or process, or training for operation of a new machine.

The Audience

Management, technical staff, production workers, the press, consumers or other clientele.

The Speaker's Purpose

To show how something works or should work, or to show the steps in a process so that the audience can use the process.

The Planning Guide

For this situation, you will need the How-To group of forms.

THE USUAL MISTAKES

Audience

Assuming that the audience knows nothing about the process, or that they know everything about it already.

Purpose And Occasion

Missing the level of purpose—showing how the *speaker* uses the process (operates the machine, for example), but not letting the *audience* learn how to do it.

Describing the process but not *showing* it.

Information Needs

Not understanding what the audience has to do with the information, or how this process fits into their day-to-day work, their decisions, etc.

Focus And Organization

Failing to break the process into steps that make it comprehensible to the audience.

Delivery

Speaking too fast, slowly, loudly, or softly.
Relying too much or too little on notes.

THE STEPS TO SUCCESS

Make It Relevant To Your Audience

Use the Audience Inventory to discover what the audience already knows about the process.

Know what they must *do* with the process: be aware of it, be able to repeat it, or be able to train others to use it.

Explain the importance of knowing the process.

Make It Complete And Documented

Give *all* steps, and give them in the right order.

Make sure the first step is really the start, and the last step is really the finish of the process.

Give the applications of the process—when and where to use it.

Make It Brief And Focused

Break the process down into a convenient number of steps.

Repetition will help, so demonstrate it three times: quickly, in the overview; in detail, in the steps; and again in the summary.

Make It Organized

Use the How-To pattern to organize your primary plan and your fallback plan.

Hand out one-page overviews of the process *before* the demonstration, and provide additional copies at the presentation.

Make It Interesting, Easy To Follow, And Polished

Plan your notes (for *both* plans) in pattern form, and at the right level of detail to suit your memory and speaking style.

Rehearse, rehearse, *rehearse*. Practice with your notes in the *actual physical setting:* standing at a podium, sitting at a table, etc. Practice with a microphone and any other props or equipment you'll actually use.

Practice the primary plan and the fallback plan.

Leave your hands free to gesture normally.

15

Giving a Report
or a Briefing

The Speaking Situation

One-way

The Place

Office, boardroom, meeting room, or setup for a press conference.

The Occasion

To bring the audience up to date on a project by announcing problems, progress, or completion.

The Audience

Management, technical staff, clients or other firms, press, and public.

The Speaker's Purpose

To give information to the people who need it or want it (or the people you *want* to want it).

The Planning Guides

For this situation, you will need the Statement-Support and Thesis-Proof groups of forms.

THE USUAL MISTAKES

Audience

Presenting 99 percent background and only one percent status or projection.

Presenting *no* background and all status or projection.

Purpose And Occasion

Not knowing how this briefing fits into the whole communication picture for this project.

Information Needs

Failing to find out what the audience already knows about the subject.

Failing to find out what the audience needs to *do* with the information (level of purpose).

Focus And Organization

Forgetting to organize the material so that the important points stand out from the mass of details.

Delivery

Speaking too fast, slowly, loudly, or softly.

Relying too much or too little on notes.

THE STEPS TO SUCCESS

Make It Relevant To Your Audience

Use the Audience Inventory to find out what your audience already knows, so that you can include the right amount of background, and then get on to present status and future projections.

Make It Complete And Documented

See how the report or briefing fits into the whole communication picture of this project.

Give the information needed for your audience to respond properly: with awareness, agreement, or action.

Make It Brief And Focused

Make the main points stand out from the details.

Focus on the present or the future, whichever is more important in this situation.

Make It Organized

Plan your notes for the primary plan and the fallback plan with a Pattern Guide.

Use a visual to *show* what you're going to *tell*.

Distribute one-page overviews before the briefing, and then provide extra copies at the presentation.

Make It Interesting, Easy To Follow, And Polished

Plan your notes (for *both* plans) in pattern form, and at the right level of detail to suit your memory and speaking style.

Rehearse, rehearse, *rehearse*. Practice with your notes in the *actual physical setting:* standing at a podium, sitting at a table, etc. Practice with a microphone and any other props or equipment you'll actually use.

Practice the primary plan and the fallback plan.

Leave your hands free to gesture normally.

16

Working in a Discussion Group or Panel

The Speaking Situation

Two-way

The Place

Office, boardroom, meeting room.

The Occasion

Regular meetings, seminars and workshops.

The Audience

Coworkers or other participants in a seminar or workshop.

The Speaker's Purpose

To help the group to set and to achieve its goals by making contributions of these types: *initiating, reacting,* and *clarifying*.

The Planning Guides

For this situation, you will need the Thesis-Proof and Opinion-Reason groups of forms.

THE USUAL MISTAKES

Audience

Thinking that the job is to sell one's own idea exclusively.
Forgetting to listen to the other speakers.
Reacting emotionally to people instead of to issues or ideas.

Purpose And Occasion

Forgetting that it's a discussion and not a lecture.
Trying to score points instead of trying to get the job done.

Information Needs

Saying what everybody already knows.
Assuming that everyone knows the background for conclusions or opinions presented.

Focus And Organization

Starting to speak without having an endpoint in mind—a statement, a re-statement, or a question.
Going off on a tangent and never coming back.

Delivery

Speaking in a tone (sarcastic, for example) which offends others or cuts off response.
Interrupting other speakers.

Loss Of Balance

Chapter 5 describes how productive groups need a balance of initiating, reacting, and clarifying behaviors. There's no perfect mix for all situations, but you, as a participant, can tell when there is too much or too little of something in your situation.

Initiating

(Too much)—jumping from one idea to the next without an opportunity to discuss any of them.

(Too little)—beating the same idea to death because nothing new is being contributed.

Reacting

(Too much)—getting carried away by emotions and reacting to people and personalities, instead of to ideas and behaviors.

(Too little)—sitting in silence, not knowing what the others think of the ideas contributed.

Clarifying

(Too much)—getting locked into an endless round of restatements and reclarifications, an intellectual gridlock.

(Too little)—steamrolling to a conclusion or a course of action before most of the group can understand the plan, the reasons, or the consequences.

THE STEPS TO SUCCESS

Make It Relevant To Your Audience

Use the Audience Inventory to understand the needs of the group.

Speak to the people who are there, and stay within the limits of the group's purposes.

Make It Complete And Documented

Give your statement or conclusions and then the basis for your views.

When you disagree, ask others for the reasons for their views.

Make It Brief And Focused

Speak briefly and then listen to responses to your ideas.

Ask for or give clarifications of points which seem vague or general.

Make It Organized

Plan your words as carefully as you would in any other speaking situation.

Use a pattern to keep a mental outline of the flow of the discussion. Write the outline as notes, if you wish.

Make It Interesting, Easy To Follow, And Polished

Smile and be friendly, even when you're disagreeing with another speaker. Look at—but don't point at—the person or people you're addressing.

Make The Group Productive

When the group is out of balance, you can help by making the right type of contribution. This is not the same as taking over the group. With these techniques you supply what is needed to restore the balance of the three types of behaviors.

Initiating

When the discussion is stagnating, contribute a new idea or a new twist to an idea being discussed.

When the group is already swimming in fifty ideas, save yours for later—wait for a better time to add it to the mix.

Reacting

When there are too many ideas to handle, pick the one you like the best and say why you like it. This will create some focus.

Respond to ideas and behaviors, but not to emotions or personalities.

Clarifying

When tempers are frayed (including yours), try to restate the *idea* being discussed. This will take the focus off the personalities.

If things are moving too fast, try to slow the pace by summarizing what has happened so far. This is easy to do if you've kept a pattern outline (Problem-Solution or Opinion-Reason) of the group's progress.

17

Brainstorming and Problem-Solving

The Speaking Situation

Two-way

The Place

Office, boardroom, or meeting room.

The Occasion

Starting up a project, reacting to a problem or other unanticipated event.

The Audience

Coworkers.

The Speaker's Purpose

To help the group explore possible solutions and then to develop an effective solution strategy.

The Planning Guides

For this situation, you will need the Problem-Solution group of forms.

THE USUAL MISTAKES

Audience

Forgetting to listen to the contributions of others.
Reacting emotionally to people instead of to issues or ideas.

Purpose And Occasion

Concentrating on arguing instead of on solving the problem.
Airing complaints in an unconstructive way.

Information Needs

Forgetting what the others already know about the problem.
Assuming that everyone knows the background for conclusions or opinions presented.

Focus And Organization

Focusing too much on the problem and not enough on a solution or solutions.
Jumping to other problems not related to the discussion.

Delivery

Telling fortunes ("That'll never work." or "I *know* this will work.").
Speaking in a tone that cuts off responses.

Loss Of Balance

Chapter 5 discusses how productive groups need a balance of initiating, reacting, and clarifying behaviors. There's no perfect mix for all situations, but you, as a participant, can tell when there is too much or too little of something in your situation.

Problem-solving is always action-oriented. Unproductive results come at two extremes:

1. The group reaches no solution.

2. The group reaches a hasty solution that is partly effective, not at all effective, or makes matters worse.

Initiating

(Too much) "Riding off in all directions" by trying to discuss all courses of action at the same time.

(Too little) Focusing too early on one action or strategy and closing off alternatives.

Reacting

(Too much) Passing judgment on ideas during brainstorming, when the purpose should be to collect ideas, not to evaluate them.

(Too little) Failing to give enough attention to each possible outcome or solution strategy.

Clarifying

(Too much) Letting two (or more) participants debate at length the exact definition or origin of a minor point.

(Too little) Allowing a solution strategy or course of action to be settled upon before exploring the plan, the reasoning behind it, and the consequences.

THE STEPS TO SUCCESS

Make It Relevant To Your Audience

Use the Audience Inventory to find out the needs of the group.

Speak to the people who are there, and use evidence that will appeal to the other participants.

Make It Complete And Documented

If you offer a solution, offer a plan to accomplish it.

When you disagree, ask others for the reasons for their views.

Make It Brief And Focused

Speak briefly, and then listen to responses to your ideas.

Ask for or give clarifications of key points that seem vague or ambiguous.

Make It Organized

Plan your words as carefully as you would in any other speaking situation.

Use a Problem-Solution outline to make a mental (or written) outline of the group's progress toward a solution.

Make It Interesting, Easy To Follow, And Polished

Smile and be friendly, even when you're disagreeing with another speaker.

Look at but don't point at the person or people you're addressing.

Make The Group Productive

When the group is out of balance, you can help by making the right type of contribution. This is not the same as taking over the group. With these techniques you supply what is needed to restore the balances of the three types of behaviors.

Initiating

During brainstorming, contribute the *possible;* don't restrict yourself to the probable.

If you bring up a new idea late in the game, introduce it by comparing it to the one or ones being discussed.

Reacting

When brainstorming is finished, pick a solution (or other idea) you favor and explain why you like it.

Keep ideas and people separate. Don't say "I don't like *your* idea," because some of the dislike becomes attached to the people involved.

Clarifying

Cool off a heated discussion by restating the ideas being discussed. This will take the focus away from the people.

When you feel a solution is being rushed, restate the group's thinking to this point. This is easy to do if you've kept a Problem-Solution outline of the group's progress.

18

Interviewing/Telephoning

The Speaking Situation

Two-way

The Place

An office.

The Occasion

Change in employment, sales call.

The Audience

Personnel manager, client.

The Speaker's Purpose

To win an employment opportunity or to make a sale.

The Planning Guides

For this situation, you will need the Opinion-Reason and Problem-Solution groups of forms.

THE USUAL MISTAKES

Audience

Not doing the homework—getting the name wrong or not knowing the person or the company.

Making the other person look bad by saying "You're wrong," or "You haven't planned well," or "You're in big trouble without me."

Purpose And Occasion

Forgetting that this is a Level-Three situation—you wouldn't be talking if you didn't want something.

Information Needs

Not knowing what the other person really wants.

Trying to sell *your* wants instead of appealing to the other person's wants.

Focus And Organization

Failing to plan the flow of ideas as you would for any other speaking situation.

Thinking all the right words will come when you get there.

Delivery

Coming on too strong, or appearing uncertain of your views.

Talking too much and not listening enough.

THE STEPS TO SUCCESS

Make It Relevant To Your Audience

Use the Audience Inventory to find out the likes and dislikes of your audience. At least discover the person's *role*.

Tailor the presentation to suit your specific audience—interviewer or client.

Make It Complete And Documented

Come prepared with everything you need to finish—to close the sale, to get the job offer.

Show how you can keep your promises. Have proof available to support your product or personal claims.

Make It Brief And Focused

Move quickly to the strongest feature of your presentation: your ability to run a department, the durability of the product, etc.

Make It Organized

Use the Opinion-Reason or Problem-Solution pattern to outline how you'd like the conversation to go.

Organize a primary plan and a fallback plan.

Make It Interesting, Easy To Follow, And Polished

Plan to let the other person talk so that you can listen for clues. Plan questions to ask to get the person talking about what you want him or her to talk about.

Make the other person feel smart. "You're right, and also . . ." will get you more sales than will "You're lucky I came along to save you."

Practice to get your timing right. Practice with another person playing the role of the interviewer or client.

Practice the primary plan and the fallback plan.

19

Debating/Arguing a Case/Negotiating

The Speaking Situation

Two-way

The Place

Office, boardroom, meeting room, and less formal settings.

The Occasion

Making a decision, settling a contract or other agreement.

The Audience

Coworkers, management, clients, vendors, family members.

The Speaker's Purpose

In debating or arguing a case, the purpose is to *win*. In business situations, however, you are not very likely to be involved in a formal debate or case argument. Negotiating, on the other hand, goes on each day—with peers, subordinates, superiors, vendors, clients, spouses, children, and anyone else with whom you must deal.

The purpose of negotiating is *to win a sensible agreement that pleases both parties, in the shortest time possible*. The rest of this Planning Guide is directed toward negotiating, but many of the same principles are involved in a formal debate or case argument.

If negotiating is going to be a large part of your job, you may want a more detailed treatment. *Getting To Yes,* by Roger Fisher and William Ury of the Harvard Negotiation Project (Houghton Mifflin, Boston, 1981), offers a complete analysis of negotiation.

The Planning Guides

For this situation, you will need the Opinion-Reason and Problem-Solution groups of forms.

THE USUAL MISTAKES

Audience

Misreading the motives of the other party.

Over- or underestimating the preparedness and the resolve of the other party.

Purpose And Occasion

Putting more energy into beating the other side than into settling with the other side.

Behaving as if toughness is the issue.

Information Needs

Failing to give the information which makes one's reasons or motives clear to the other party.

Not listening for clues to position and motives.

Focus And Organization

Not knowing the real needs or wants of the side you represent.

Focusing on just one part of the package and forgetting the rest.

Delivery

Speaking in a sarcastic or belligerent tone.

Conveying through body language the messages "I'm not listening to you" or "I don't care what you say."

The Means To The Ends—Strategy

Setting no standards for success *before* negotiating.

Having no plan except to react to the other party's plan.

Starting with unrealistic demands.

Planning to take all but not to give an inch.

Failing to make a fallback plan to use if objectives are unreachable with the primary plan.

The Means To The Ends—Tactics

Talking too much about "you want" and "I want" and not enough about what is realistic, fair, workable, achievable, or best for everybody.

Hanging on to the primary plan after it is clear that it isn't working.

Giving something without getting something in return, or failing to explain why you're making a concession.

Threatening an ultimatum that can't be backed up.

Cutting off discussion in anger.

THE STEPS TO SUCCESS

Make It Relevant To Your Audience

Use the Audience Inventory to discover the wants and needs of the other side so that you can address them.

Justify your own case with arguments that appeal to the other party.

Make It Complete And Documented

Give data to support your arguments: costs, rates, profit margins, hours required, etc.

Come fully prepared to work toward a general agreement and specific details.

Make It Brief And Focused

Tell what's in it for the other side by zeroing in on their primary needs.

Make your point quickly and then give the evidence.

Respond to their points in short counter-proposals.

Make It Organized

See the big picture and set each bargaining point into that context.

Give an overview of your points before you present any in detail. Decide which, if any, to keep in reserve.

From time to time, summarize the progress made toward agreement.

Make It Interesting, Easy To Follow, And Polished

Rehearse, rehearse, *rehearse*. Practice with someone playing the role of the other spokesperson.

Practice the primary plan and the fallback plan.

Use your plan to keep you on track.

The Means To The Ends—Strategy

Set the standards for success—the goals you want to achieve—*before* the first session.

Make a plan that begins with needs and then moves toward means of satisfying these needs.

Know your alternatives (second and third choices) for each major point, and make them the basis for your fallback plan.

Anticipate the arguments, evidence, and possible demands or positions of the other party, and prepare responses.

Assume that you'll compromise, and look for the common ground, a mutual solution rather than a victory.

Plan to keep notes on your progress toward a settlement.

The Means To The Ends—Tactics

When it makes sense to concede, explain why you're willing to concede, and suggest an area of concession from the other part.

From time to time, compare your notes on progress with your primary plan to see if it's working.

Try to end every session on a point of agreement. The last few minutes of a bargaining session can be like the two-minute drill in a football game: you might well settle more in the last two minutes than you did in the other hours of marching back and forth.

Look for every area of agreement. An agreement on principle is better than no agreement at all, because it puts the next session in a positive light.

20

Forms

THE FIVE GROUPS OF FORMS IN THIS CHAPTER MAY BE PHOTOCOPIED AND USED for the speaking situations given in chapters 11 through 19. Each new form begins on a right-hand page for easier use. As stated previously, if you would like the forms to fit on $8^{1}/_{2}$- × -11-inch paper, you will want to photocopy them at 129 percent.

STATEMENT-SUPPORT

AUDIENCE INVENTORY

*Type of Presentation:*_____

*Size and Makeup of Audience:*_____

1. Who are these people? What is their background in this business or technical area?

2. What is their experience in this area?

3. What are their special interests? What do they want from me?

4. What are my purposes? What do I want to give them?

5. How can I match up these wants lists?

***

6. What do they know about the company (or other group) I represent?

7. What do they know about my background, experience, and professional reputation?

***

8. How are they likely to react to my ideas on this issue or proposal? Will they be likely to agree? To what extent?

9. What kinds of evidence would be most convincing to them?

10. What level of detail should be included?

***

11. How are they accustomed to getting information? How long will they want to listen?

12. How would they want the material organized? Where would they want me to begin?

***

13. What do they have to be able to do on the basis of the information and arguments I present?

14. Should they be aware of a trend? Able to draw a conclusion? Able to make a decision?

***

15. What questions will they be likely to ask?

PATTERN GUIDE
Statement-Support—Level One

Statement   (Gives an overview and states the most important point)

Support #1   (The first block of details to support the statement)

Support #2   (The next block of details)

Support #3   (The last block or blocks of supporting details)

Application   (Summarizes and then tells how the information can be used)

SPECIAL TACTICS FOR CRUCIAL POINTS

I will show them my plan and keep them on track by:

_____ Giving an Overview

_____ Using a Printed Handout

_____ Using a Graphic or Visual

Notes and text for tactic chosen

I will create focus with the first words by:

_____ Using a Focus Object

_____ Using Deliberate Silence

_____ Using an Anecdote, Fable, or Story

_____ Using a Famous Quotation

_____ Cooking Up a Surprise

_____ Using Repetition

Notes and text for tactic chosen

I will finish strong with the last words by:

_____ Repeating and Extending the Opening

_____ Giving a Before-and-After Picture

_____ Looking to the Future

_____ Offering a Challenge

Notes and text for tactic chosen

EVALUATION CHECKLIST
Statement-Support—Level One

The Situation

_____ Did you find out exactly what you're hired to do?

_____ Do you know the significance of the occasion?

_____ Did you use the Inventory to find the audience's information needs?

_____ Do you know your purpose—exactly what you want from this audience?

_____ Do you know the actual physical setting of your presentation?

Revising Plan for Situation

Statement

_____ Does your opening focus the audience's attention on your main idea?

_____ Have you given an overview which shows your destination and route?

_____ Have you stated your main point in terms your audience can understand?

Revising Plan for Statement

Support #1

_____ Have you developed this support in sufficient detail?

_____ Have you linked this support to the statement and other supports?

Revising Plan for Support #1

Support #2

_____ Have you developed this support in enough detail to make it interesting?

_____ Have you related this support to the rest of the presentation?

Revising Plan for Support #2

Support #3

_____ Is the support developed in enough detail to be clear and interesting?

_____ Have you related this final support (or supports) to your statement? to the other supports?

Revising Plan for Support #3

Application

_____ Have you given a summary of your main points so far?

_____ Have you shown the value of this information to your audience?

_____ Did you relate this topic to other topics that might be of interest to your audience?

_____ Do your last words leave the audience with your most important point?

Revising Plan for Application

Delivery

_____ Have you prepared speaking notes for the actual physical setting?

_____ Have you written out the first sentence and the last sentence?

_____ Have you rehearsed *aloud* with your notes in the actual setting?

_____ Have you rehearsed with a microphone, lectern, overhead projector, props, and every other piece of equipment you'll use?

_____ Have you planned your attire to set the tone for the situation and purpose?

_____ Have you prepared and rehearsed a fallback plan?

Revising Plan for Delivery

THESIS-PROOF

AUDIENCE INVENTORY

Type of Presentation _____

Size and Makeup of Audience _____

1. Who are these people? What is their background in this business or technical area?

2. What is their experience in this area?

3. What are their special interests—what do they want from me?

4. What are my purposes—what do I want to give them?

5. How can I match up these wants lists?

***

6. What do they know about the company (or other group) I represent?

7. What do they know about my background, experience, and professional reputation?

***

8. How are they likely to react to my ideas on this issue or proposal? Will they be likely to agree? To what extent?

9. What kinds of evidence would be most convincing to them?

10. What level of detail should be included?

***

11. How are they accustomed to getting information? How long will they want to listen?

12. How would they want the material organized? Where would they want me to begin?

***

13. What do they have to be able to do on the basis of the information and arguments I present?

14. Should they be aware of a trend? Able to draw a conclusion? Able to make a decision?

***

15. What questions will they be likely to ask?

PATTERN GUIDE
Thesis-Proof—Level Two

Thesis   (Gives overview and states main point to be proven)

Proof #1   (Gives the first block of evidence)

Proof #2   (The next block of evidence)

Proof #3   (The last block or blocks of evidence)

Significance   (Summarizes and then shows impact or effects on audience)

SPECIAL TACTICS FOR CRUCIAL POINTS

I will show them my plan and keep them on track by:

_____   Giving an Overview

_____   Using a Printed Handout

_____   Using a Graphic or Visual

Notes and text for tactic chosen

I will create focus with the first words by:

_____   Using a Focus Object

_____   Using Deliberate Silence

_____   Using an Anecdote, Fable or Story

_____   Using a Famous Quotation

_____   Cooking Up a Surprise

_____   Using Repetition

Notes and text for tactic chosen

I will finish strong with the last words by:

_____   Repeating and Extending the Opening

_____   Giving a Before-and-After Picture

_____   Looking to the Future

_____   Offering a Challenge

Notes and text for tactic chosen

EVALUATION CHECKLIST
Thesis-Proof—Level Two

The Situation

_____ Did you find out exactly what you're hired to do?

_____ Do you know the significance of the occasion?

_____ Did you use the Inventory to find the audience's information needs?

_____ Do you know your purpose—exactly what you want from this audience?

_____ Do you know the actual physical setting of your presentation?

Revising Plan for Situation

Thesis

_____ Does your opening focus the audience's attention on your main idea?

_____ Have you stated your thesis so that the audience can understand what you're trying to prove?

_____ Have you accounted for the audience's likely reactions to your view?

Revising Plan for Thesis

Proof #1

_____ Does this proof include evidence that will be convincing to your audience?

_____ Have you shown the logical connection between this proof and your thesis?

_____ Is the proof developed in enough detail to be forceful?

Revising Plan for Proof #1

Proof #2

_____ Have you developed this second proof in enough detail to have impact?

_____ Have you related this proof to the thesis? To the other proofs?

Revising Plan for Proof #2

Proof #3

_____ Does this final proof (or proofs) complete your argument?

_____ Have you developed this final proof effectively?

_____ Have you related it to earlier proofs? To the thesis? To the significance?

Revising Plan for Proof #3

Significance

_____ Have you given a summary of your main points so far?

_____ Have you led the audience to the conclusions you want?

_____ Have you identified the effects or results they might expect?

_____ Have you made your final point effectively? Do your last words really close the presentation?

Revising Plan for Significance

Delivery

_____ Have you prepared speaking notes for the actual physical setting?

_____ Have you written out the first sentence and the last sentence?

_____ Have you rehearsed aloud with your notes in the actual setting?

_____ Have you rehearsed with a microphone, lectern, overhead projector, props, and every other piece of equipment you'll use?

_____ Have you planned your attire to set the tone for the situation and purpose?

_____ Have you prepared and rehearsed a fallback plan?

Revising Plan for Delivery

OPINION-REASON

THE AUDIENCE INVENTORY

Type of Presentation _____

Size and Makeup of Audience _____

1. Who are these people? What is their background in this business or technical area?

2. What is their experience in this area?

3. What are their special interests—what do they want from me?

4. What are my purposes—what do I want to give them?

5. How can I match up these wants lists?

***

6. What do they know about the company (or other group) I represent?

7. What do they know about my background, experience, and professional reputation?

***

8. How are they likely to react to my ideas on this issue or proposal? Will they be likely to agree? To what extent?

9. What kinds of evidence would be most convincing to them?

10. What level of detail should be included?

***

11. How are they accustomed to getting information? How long will they want to listen?

12. How would they want the material organized? Where would they want me to begin?

***

13. What do they have to be able to do on the basis of the information and arguments I present?

14. Should they be aware of a trend? Able to draw a conclusion? Able to make a
    decision?

***

15. What questions will they be likely to ask?

PATTERN GUIDE
Opinion-Reason—Level Three

Opinion   (Gives overview and focuses on main opinion to be stated)

Reason #1   (The first block of evidence to justify the opinion)

Reason #2   (The second block of evidence)

Reason #3   (The last block or blocks of supporting evidence)

Recommendation   (Summarizes and gives plan for action based on the opinion)

SPECIAL TACTICS FOR CRUCIAL POINTS

I will show them my plan and keep them on track by:

_____ Giving an Overview

_____ Using a Printed Handout

_____ Using a Graphic or Visual

Notes and text for tactic chosen

I will create focus with the first words by:

_____ Using a Focus Object

_____ Using Deliberate Silence

_____ Using an Anecdote, Fable or Story

_____ Using a Famous Quotation

_____ Cooking Up a Surprise

_____ Using Repetition

Notes and text for tactic chosen

I will finish strong with the last words by:

_____ Repeating and Extending the Opening

_____ Giving a Before-and-After Picture

_____ Looking to the Future

_____ Offering a Challenge

Notes and text for tactic chosen

EVALUATION CHECKLIST
Opinion-Reason—Level Three

The Situation

_____ Did you find out exactly what you're hired to do?

_____ Do you know the significance of the occasion?

_____ Did you use the Inventory to find the audience's information needs?

_____ Do you know your purpose—exactly what you want from this audience?

_____ Do you know the actual physical setting of your presentation?

Revising Plan for Situation

Opinion

_____ Do you immediately focus the audience's attention on your main idea?

_____ Have you given an overview which shows your destination and route?

_____ Have you stated your opinion so that the audience will know exactly where you stand?

_____ Have you accounted for the audience's likely reactions to your opinion?

Revising Plan for Opinion

Reason #1

_____ Have you shown how this reason should have value for your audience?

_____ Have you given your reason enough development to make it convincing?

_____ Have you related this reason to your opinion?

Revising Plan for Reason #1

Reason #2

_____ Did you show the relevance of this part of the argument to your audience?

_____ Have you given enough detail to be clear and convincing?

Revising Plan for Reason #2

Reason #3

_____ Is this third reason (and any additional reasons) directly connected to the other reasons? To the opinion?

_____ Have you given a summary of what has come before?

Revising Plan for Reason #3

Recommendation

_____ Have you given a summary of the main points so far?

_____ Have you told the audience what to do and how to go about it?

_____ Have you explained the benefits of carrying out your recommendation?

_____ Have you given enough motivation for action?

_____ Does the last sentence leave the audience with your most important point? Have you made a graceful but forceful exit?

Revising Plan for Recommendation

Delivery

_____ Have you prepared speaking notes for the actual physical setting?

_____ Have you written out the first sentence and the last sentence?

_____ Have you rehearsed aloud with your notes in the actual setting?

_____ Have you rehearsed with a microphone, lectern, overhead projector, props, and every other piece of equipment you'll use?

_____ Have you planned your attire to set the tone for the situation and purpose?

_____ Have you prepared and rehearsed a fallback plan?

Revising Plan for Delivery

PROBLEM-SOLUTION

THE AUDIENCE INVENTORY

Type of Presentation _____

Size and makeup of Audience _____

1. Who are these people? What is their background in this business or technical area?

2. What is their experience in this area?

3. What are their special interests—what do they want from me?

4. What are my purposes—what do I want to give them?

5. How can I match up these wants lists?

***

6. What do they know about the company (or other group) I represent?

7. What do they know about my background, experience, and professional reputation?

***

8. How are they likely to react to my ideas on this issue or proposal? Will they be likely to agree? To what extent?

9. What kinds of evidence would be most convincing to them?

10. What level of detail should be included?

***

11. How are they accustomed to getting information? How long will they want to listen?

12. How would they want the material organized? Where would they want me to begin?

***

13. What do they have to be able to do on the basis of the information and arguments I present?

14. Should they be aware of a trend? Able to draw a conclusion? Able to make a decision?

***

15. What questions will they be likely to ask?

PATTERN GUIDE
Problem-Solution—Level Three

Problem   (Gives overview and defines the scope of the problem to be solved)

Effects   (Shows the severity of impact of the problem)

Causes   (Traces the problem's causes)

Solution   (Gives a plan for action)

Significance   (Tells what benefits will result from using this solution)

SPECIAL TACTICS FOR CRITICAL POINTS

I will show them my plan and keep them on track by:

_____ Giving an Overview

_____ Using a Printed Handout

_____ Using a Graphic or Visual

Notes and text for tactic chosen

I will create focus with the first words by:

_____ Using a Focus Object

_____ Using Deliberate Silence

_____ Using an Anecdote, Fable or Story

_____ Using a Famous Quotation

_____ Cooking Up a Surprise

_____ Using Repetition

Notes and text for tactic chosen

I will finish strong with the last words by:

_____ Repeating and Extending the Opening

_____ Giving a Before-and-After Picture

_____ Looking to the Future

_____ Offering a Challenge

Notes and text for tactic chosen

EVALUATION CHECKLIST
Problem-Solution—Level Three

The Situation

_____ Did you find out exactly what you're hired to do?

_____ Do you know the significance of the occasion?

_____ Did you use the Inventory to find the audience's information needs?

_____ Do you know your purpose—exactly what you want from this audience?

_____ Do you know the actual physical setting of your presentation?

Revising Plan for Situation

Problem

_____ Does your opening focus the audience's attention on your main idea?

_____ Have you given an overview which shows your destination and route?

_____ Have you clearly shown the limits of the problem—how big, how much, how many, how long—in terms your audience can understand?

Revising Plan for Problem

Effects

_____ Have you illustrated the most dramatic or important effects?

_____ Have you focused on a few effects instead of trying to list dozens?

_____ Have you shown your audience how they will be affected?

Revising Plan for Effects

Causes

_____ Have you given the most important cause or causes? Did you need to rule out other possible causes to isolate the ones you've identified?

_____ Have you given sufficient evidence to establish these causes?

_____ Have you directly related the causes to the problem and effects?

Revising Plan for Causes

Solution

_____ Is your solution strategy clear and specific?

_____ Have you given enough detail to show how the solution will work?

_____ Have you told the audience what you want them to think or to do?

_____ Have you linked the solution to the causes? To the significance?

_____ Have you given a summary of your main points so far?

Revising Plan for Solution

Significance

_____ Have you shown all of the benefits of your solution—the long-range benefits as well as the short-range or immediate ones?

_____ Have you identified what individuals and groups will benefit?

_____ Do your final words really finish the presentation? This is your last chance with the audience. Have you made an effective closing?

Revising Plan for Significance

Delivery

_____ Have you prepared speaking notes for the actual physical setting?

_____ Have you written out the first sentence and the last sentence?

_____ Have you rehearsed aloud with your notes in the actual setting?

_____ Have you rehearsed with a microphone, lectern, overhead projector, props, and every other piece of equipment you'll use?

_____ Have you planned your attire to set the tone for the situation and purpose?

_____ Have you prepared and rehearsed a fallback plan?

Revising Plan for Delivery

HOW-TO

THE AUDIENCE INVENTORY

Type of Presentation _____

Size and Makeup of Audience _____

1. Who are these people? What is their background in this business or technical area?

2. What is their experience in this area?

3. What are their special interests—what do they want from me?

4. What are my purposes—what do I want to give them?

5. How can I match up these wants lists?

***

6. What do they know about the company (or other group) I represent?

7. What do they know about my background, experience, and professional reputation?

***

8. How are they likely to react to my ideas on this issue or proposal? Will they be likely to agree? To what extent?

9. What kinds of evidence would be most convincing to them?

10. What level of detail should be included?

***

11. How are they accustomed to getting information? How long will they want to listen?

12. How would they want the material organized? Where would they want me to begin?

***

13. What do they have to be able to do on the basis of the information and arguments I present?

14. Should they be aware of a trend? Able to draw a conclusion? Able to make a decision?

***

15. What questions will they be likely to ask?

PATTERN GUIDE
How-To—Level Two

Motivation   (Gives an overview and tells the importance of knowing the process)

Step #1   (Shows the first step in the process)

Step #2   (Shows the next step)

Step #3   (Shows the last step or steps)

Application   (Summarizes and shows how and when the process should be
used)

SPECIAL TACTICS FOR CRUCIAL POINTS

I will show them my plan and keep them on track by:

_____ Giving an Overview

_____ Using a Printed Handout

_____ Using a Graphic or Visual

Notes and text for tactic chosen

I will create focus with the first words by:

_____ Using a Focus Object

_____ Using Deliberate Silence

_____ Using an Anecdote, Fable or Story

_____ Using a Famous Quotation

_____ Cooking Up a Surprise

_____ Using Repetition

Notes and text for tactic chosen

I will finish strong with the last words by:

_____ Repeating and Extending the Opening

_____ Giving a Before-and-After Picture

_____ Looking to the Future

_____ Offering a Challenge

Notes and text for tactic chosen

EVALUATION CHECKLIST
How-To—Level Two

The Situation

_____ Did you find out exactly what you're hired to do?

_____ Do you know the significance of the occasion?

_____ Did you use the Inventory to find the audience's information needs?

_____ Do you know your purpose—exactly what you want from this audience?

_____ Do you know the actual physical setting of your presentation?

Revising Plan for Situation

Motivation

_____ Does your opening focus the audience's attention on the main idea?

_____ Have you shown the value to your audience of knowing this process?

_____ Have you given an overview which shows your destination and route?

_____ Did you list the main steps?

Revising Plan for Motivation

Step #1

_____ Have you explained why this step should come first?

_____ Have you given the necessary background for this first step? Could someone follow these directions?

Revising Plan for Step #1

Step #2

_____ Have you shown this second step clearly and completely?

_____ Have you shown the relation of this step to the other steps?

Revising Plan for Step #2

Step #3

_____ Have you explained the last step in enough detail to make it clear?

_____ Have you related this step (or steps) to the earlier steps?

Revising Plan for Step #3

Application

_____ Have you given a summary of the main points so far?

_____ Have you shown the uses or applications of the process?

_____ Did you tell how and when the process should be used?

_____ Are there any special warnings, suggestions, or other bits of advice?

_____ Do your last words leave the audience with your most important point?

Revising Plan for Application

Delivery

_____ Have you prepared speaking notes for the actual physical setting?

_____ Have you written out the first sentence and the last sentence?

_____ Have you rehearsed aloud with your notes in the actual setting?

_____ Have you rehearsed with a microphone, lectern, overhead projector, props, and every other piece of equipment you'll use?

_____ Have you planned your attire to set the tone for the situation and purpose?

_____ Have you prepared and rehearsed a fallback plan?

Revising Plan for Delivery

Index